Coincraft's Coin Checklist

1656-1816

Richard Lobel
Allan Hailstone
Eleni Calligas

COINCRAFT

London 1999

First published in 1999
by Standard Catalogue Publishers for
Coincraft
44 & 45 Great Russell Street
London WC1B 3LU

© Richard Lobel 1999

All rights reserved

British Library Cataloguing in Publication Data
A catalogue record for this book is available from the British Library

ISBN 0 9526228 58

Database typeset by Polestar Whitefriars Ltd
Printed and bound by Polestar Wheatons Ltd

Contents

Glossary 5
Five Guineas 59
Fifty Shillings 62
Two Guineas 63
Broad 65
Guinea 66
Half Guinea 72
Third Guinea 77
Quarter Guinea 78
Crown 79
Double Florin 84
Three Shillings 85
Halfcrown 86
Eighteen Pence Bank Token 93
Shilling 94
Sixpence 101
Maundy Fourpence 106
Silver Threepence 109
Silver Twopence 112
Silver Penny 116
Copper/Bronze Penny 119
Halfpenny 120
Farthing 124
Proof Set 128

Hello & Welcome!

Welcome to *Coincraft's Coin Checklist, 1656–1816*. This second volume will complete our coverage of the English and UK milled coinage from 1656 to date. Of course, when describing coins, the term 'milled' is a misnomer as the differentiation is between machine-struck instead of hammered coins, irrespective of whether they bear a milled edge. Nevertheless, it is the term which the general collecting public accepts and so we will use it.

You will see that in the *Checklist* there is an entry for every coin from 1656 to 1816 listed in *Coincraft's Standard Catalogue of English & UK Coins, 1066 to Date*. Each Checklist entry has the coin's CSC number followed by the date of issue and a features column with information that will help distinguish between coins of the same date. The rest of the entry is for you to fill in so that you build a full acquisition record for every coin you buy or are given. There is a small box that you can use either to indicate that you own a coin or to compile a 'wants list'. There is also space for noting the grade of a coin you bought, who you bought it from, the date of purchase and the price you paid. The final column allows you to note the value of the coin today, which is particularly useful when you want to insure your collection.

The Checklists constitute an important part of a coin collection and can be used in a variety of ways.

The first volume of our *Checklist* covers English and UK coins from 1816 to date and is available from any good coin shop, book shop or directly from Coincraft. It is the same size and format as this one, contains over 120 pages and costs £6.95. Together, the two books cover all the British & English milled series from 1656 to date.

Stay well, be happy and keep on collecting.

Richard Lobel

Glossary

Aberystwyth Mint The first provincial mint to be established by Charles I. It was opened in Wales in 1638 by Sir Thomas Bushell, the lessee of the Welsh silver mines. His privy mark was an open book. Coins were struck at this mint from dies shipped in from London and their minting ceased before the Civil War started.

Adjustment Marks When a flan or planchet was too heavy for a particular denomination, an adjuster would scrape it by hand to bring it down to the correct weight.

AE Symbol for 'aes', an abbreviation for copper or bronze.

After Union Coins struck during the reign of Queen Anne after the Union of England and Scotland in 1707. Those struck at Edinburgh can be distinguished by an E or E* below the bust. Only silver coins are known with an E or E*.

Altered Date Where the date on a coin has been changed. Sometimes mints reuse dies and punch or re-engrave a new date over an old date. In some cases a coin will be altered unofficially to increase its collector value. An example is the 1933 penny, altered from 1935 into 1933.

Angel An English gold coin first issued in 1465 with a value of 6 shillings and 8 pence. St Michael spearing a dragon is on the obverse and a ship on the reverse. This denomination was struck under every monarch until the reign of Charles I.

Anglo-Hanoverian Coinage When Georg Ludwig became king of England in 1714, he retained his German dukedom of Brunswick-Lüneberg in north central Germany -the name of which changed to Hanover in 1814 when it became a kingdom. Thus, George I, George II, George III, George IV and William IV were rulers of both Brunswick-Lüneberg (Hanover) and the United Kingdom. As a result, coins of Brunswick-Lüneberg issued between 1714 and 1837, though on a German standard and naturally showing German elements in the design, often portray the British monarchs, as well as their British regal titles and even, sometimes, the British coat of arms. On the accession of Victoria, due to Salic law which forbids the accession of a woman, the kingdom of Hanover passed to the Duke of Cumberland.

Annulet A ring, usually very small, in many cases used as a mintmark. Henry VI's coinage can be dated according to the placement of the annulet.

Coincraft's Coin Checklist

Ansell Sovereign — Sovereigns struck in 1859 by the Royal Mint under G.F. Ansell to test the use of Australian gold. The gold proved too brittle for use in coinage. An Ansell sovereign can be distinguished by the line down the ribbon or tie in Victoria's hair.

Anson, Admiral — Admiral Anson circumnavigated the globe and brought back silver and gold which he had captured from the Spanish, but not off Lima, Peru. The coins that were struck by George II with Lima below his bust might indicate that the coins captured carried the Lima mintmark.

AR — Denotes *Argentum*, i.e. silver.

Artificially Toned — A coin which has been treated in some way to simulate a natural toning or give the appearance of age. It is sometimes done to disguise a badly cleaned coin. The colour is often very dark and somewhat lifeless. In some cases it can be rubbed away simply by touching the coin.

Assay — A test to determine the actual metal content of an object or coin, i.e. the fineness of the precious metal as a percentage of the total content.

AU — A grade which is designated as About Uncirculated.

Au — Denotes *Aurum*, i.e. gold.

Bag Marks — When coins are struck they are placed in bags and then moved to the place where they will be distributed to the public for everyday use. In that moving the coins rub up against each other and acquire small marks; these are called bag marks. The fewer the number and the less severity of the marks the higher the value of the coin.

Bank of England Dollar — Struck from 1804 until about 1814 but still retaining the date 1804. It was issued by the Bank of England to help alleviate the shortage of change, and overstruck on eight reales of the Spanish world to replace the countermarked coins. Previously a punch which had been used to hallmark silver with George III's portrait was used to countermark Spanish dollars and make them legal tender. A wit in those days said it was 'the head of an ass on the head of a fool'.

Bank Token — Issued by the Bank of England between 1811 and 1816, they were struck in silver with denominations of (a) one shilling and sixpence and (b) three shillings. The Bank's name does not appear on the coins, just the legend 'Bank Token'. There is also a pattern ninepence token known. From the condition of many of these Bank Tokens they saw considerable circulation.

Glossary

Barton's Metal — A very thin layer of gold which is laminated or bonded to a copper blank.

Base Metal — A non-precious metal, i.e. not silver, gold, platinum, or palladium. Usually copper or bronze but today it also includes aluminium, stainless steel and cupro-nickel.

Bath Metal — A mixture of zinc (24.7%), copper (75%) and silver (0.3%), it is named after the city of Bath where it was invented. It was used in the 1720s to make coins for the American Colonies.

Beading — The small dots sometimes found either around the rim of a coin or between the legend and a field.

Before Union — Coin struck in the reign of Queen Anne before the union of England and Scotland in 1707.

Bell Metal — Originally referred to coins struck from the melted church bells of France.

Bi-metallic — A coin which is made up of two separate metals. In modern coins, they are usually in concentric circles. The James II tin coinage had a brass plug inserted in it to help stop counterfeiting.

Billon — A mixture of silver and another metal where the silver makes up a maximum of 50% of the mixture. When first issued and still shiny from the mint, a billon coin will look like silver, but paler. After wear the other metal comes through and the coin will look coppery. The posthumous coinage of Henry VIII is a good example of what can happen and the reason he got the nickname 'Copper Nose'.

Blacksmith Half Crown — A crude halfcrown struck in Kilkenny in Ireland during the Civil War. This is a very rare copy of the Tower Mint halfcrown.

Blank — The metal disc, also called a planchet or flan, upon which the design of the coin is impressed. The blank is fed into a press where extreme pressure causes the metal of the blank to flow into the reversed design of the dies so the design comes out raised.

Blondeau, Pierre — A French engraver who worked at the Tower Mint during the Commonwealth administration and Charles II's reign. He reintroduced the screw press for the making of milled or machine struck coins. It had not been used since Elizabeth I was on the throne. He also had the ability to put inscriptions or lettering on a coin's edge. This lettering was first used by Blondeau on pattern coins of 1651. It was not until 1658 that this process was regularly used on crowns and, after 1668, on five guineas. A lettered edge stopped the clipping of coins.

Coincraft's Coin Checklist

Blundered Inscription It will appear on a coin which has been struck several times and the slight shifting has made the legend unreadable.

Bob Slang term for shilling.

Bonnet Piece A gold coin issued under James V of Scotland, it was valued at one ducat (3.5 grams). It was struck in 1539 from gold found at Crawford Muir. It is the first Scottish coin to bear a date.

Border The outer part of a coin nearest to the edge and rim. Usually part of the design and used to ensure that the coin will wear better and longer.

Boulton, Matthew (1728-1809) A manufacturer of coinage machinery, from Birmingham. Most famous for his Soho Mint which issued many of the early copper coins of George III, including the famous Cartwheel twopence and penny, as well as the Bank of England dollar. Boulton was the first person to use steam power to strike coins.

Brass Threepence A denomination which was struck for circulation from 1937 until 1967 and then in the 1970 Proof Set. The twelve-sided coin was first designed for issue under Edward VIII and after he abdicated it bore the portrait of George VI.

Breeches Money A slang term for the coinage under the Commonwealth. The two shields looked like an inflated pair of men's breeches.

Brilliant Uncirculated A condition of grading. On copper and bronze coins it means bright and shiny just as they came from the mint. On silver coins it means with little or no toning, perhaps the middle coins from a roll where the outer coins have toned.

Briot, Nicholas (1580-1646) Arrived in England ca 1626 and believed in machine struck coinage. A superb engraver, perhaps the finest this country has ever known. His work was far superior to the crude coins that were being struck at that time. During the Civil War he was loyal to Charles I and worked at York and Oxford. His coinage is neat, precise and most attractive.

Britain Crown A five shilling gold coin issued by James I in 1604. The legend reads HENRICUS ROSAS REGNA JACOBUS (Henry unites the roses, James the kingdoms)

Britannia Groat William IV reintroduced the groat into general circulation. It had not been in regular use since Charles I. His new groat had the seated figure of Britannia on it; the final issue was the Jubilee issue of Victoria in 1888, which was struck exclusively for British Guinea.

Glossary

Britannia Her seated figure can first be seen on Roman coins under Hadrian and Antoninius Pius which were struck to commemorate their victories in the British dominions. Britannia is now depicted seated on a rock with a shield and trident in her hand.

Broad A gold piece to the value of twenty shillings struck with the portrait of Oliver Cromwell, engraved by Thomas Simon and dated 1656.

Brockage When a coin is stuck in a die and another planchet is introduced, that first coin makes an incused impression on the second coin. It acts like a miniature die. The second coin ends up with the same impression raised and incused.

Bronzed Copper coins which have been covered with a thin layer of bronze, usually on proof coins to make them more attractive.

Bull Head The portrait depicting George III on the new halfcrown after the Currency Reform Act of 1816. It was only used in 1816 and 1817. While some collectors also use this term to describe the shilling and sixpence of this issue, I have my doubts. After all it was only the design of the halfcrown which was changed in 1817.

Bullion Coin A coin which changes hands at or near its intrinsic value. In recent years usually struck and sold for the hoarding of precious metal. They are of no numismatic value except curiosity value. Some coins which sell at 'gold' or 'silver value' were legitimate issues: sovereigns, French 20 francs etc.

Bun Coinage The bronze coinage of Queen Victoria with a youthful portrait and her hair tied up in a bun; it was issued from 1860-1895.

Bungtown Coppers Imitations of British copper coins struck mainly in the United Kingdom and also the American Colonies. There were many counterfeits of copper halfpennies, a number with most amusing legends. Also known as *Regal evasions*.

Bushell, Thomas The lessee of the North Wales silver mines. In 1637 Charles I gave him permission to strike coins at Aberystwyth. These coins have the Welsh plumes and a privy mark of an open book. The quality of the engraving is quite fine and the workmanship extremely neat. They are beautiful coins.

Cabinet Friction If coins are kept and displayed in wooden cabinets they tend to move about when the tray is taken out and rubbing or friction often occurs on the high points. These coins might not have seen circulation but unfortunately the cabinet friction does adversely affect their value.

Coincraft's Coin Checklist

Calais This French town came under English rule in 1363-1412 and again from 1424 to about 1440. English silver and gold coins were struck there and either have the legend VILLA CALESIE (many varieties exist) or a 'C' mintmark.

Carlisle, Siege Issues Carlisle, a town on the borders of England and Scotland, was besieged during the Civil War. From October 1644 to June 1645, octagonal shaped coins were struck there from dinner plates made of silver. The coins were valued at one and three shillings.

Cartouche A scroll-like ornamental design, usually containing some feature within it, e.g. the lion at the centre of the William III crown reverse.

Cartwheel A slang name for the copper coinage of 1797. The Soho Mint issued one and two penny coins which weighed one and two ounces respectively (28.35 and 56.7 grams). It was the only time a government tried to give value for money. As expected, the public hated the heavy two pence and the famous Cartwheel twopence was never issued again. The penny was actually struck for a number of years but all the coins bear the date 1797.

Cased Set A group of coins which is issued in some sort of casing or packaging. They are usually all of the same date and made other than for general circulation. They can be issued for a coronation, jubilee or the like.

Chevron Milling A 'V' shaped milling introduced to deter counterfeiting on the gold coinage of George II and George III.

Choice Uncirculated A grade. A coin is Uncirculated if it has never been in circulation and is without wear. But due to the vagaries of how coins are struck, how the dies were made and how the coins were treated after striking, there are different grades of Uncirculated. Choice Uncirculated is better than a normal Uncirculated coin with far fewer bag marks and is well struck with full and uninterrupted lustre.

Clash Marks The marks made on one die when it is struck by the other die without a flan or blank in between. When coins are struck from that die, they will have a minor impression from both dies.

Glossary

Clipping The process by which a quantity of metal was unofficially removed from the edge of a coin, which would then be passed on for its original value. People would also take hammered coins, put them in a sack, then shake the sack vigorously for hours. The sack would then be melted down and any metal left would be the person's wages for the day. This was called 'sweating' the coins. It was illegal, but in the reign of Elizabeth I as long as the inner circle was not broken, the coin was still legal tender.

Coin Weight A piece of metal which exactly reproduces the weight of a known coin. This is used to check if a coin is of the proper weight and fineness. The coin goes in one side of a balance scale and the weight in the other; if the coin is of the correct weight then the scale will balance.

Coin A form of money, today the fractional part of a paper note. Usually round and struck in metal, but there have been square, triangular and other shapes also struck. In the 7th Century BC the first stamped piece of metal was issued in Lydia.

Collar The metal ring which retains the blank while a coin is being struck. A collar can also impart a lettering or design on the edge of a coin whilst it is being struck.

Commemorative A coin struck to honour or commemorate an event or person. In the past many commemoratives were issued at or near their face value. Today they are usually issued for collectors and to produce revenue for the issuing country or marketer. Many of the commemoratives issued today are not issued for general circulation and thus are *NCLT* (Non Circulating Legal Tender).

Condor Token Privately issued copper tokens to the value of a farthing, halfpenny or penny in the late 1700s. First issued by the Parys Mining Company in Wales. Due to the shortage of small change they were readily accepted as money and rapidly spread all over the country. The merchants made a small profit on the manufacture of the tokens and also advertised their wares for free on the tokens. The first widely used book on this subject was written by James Condor and thus they are often referred to as Condor Tokens.

Conjoined Two or more busts shown slightly overlapping and looking in the same direction.

Contemporary Forgery A copy of coin made during the time that the coin circulated.

Coincraft's Coin Checklist

Copper Nose — A nickname given to Henry VIII whose posthumous coinage was so debased that, when it became worn, the copper showed through on Henry's nose. Thus he became known as 'Old Copper Nose'.

Copper-nickel — See *Cupro-nickel*.

Copy — A reproduction of something, in this case a coin. Museums make copies, some for their own collection and some for sale in their shops. Over the years some copies have become very collectable. For example the Renaissance copies of Roman coins known as Paduans are highly collected. Modern copies are often made to deceive collectors.

Corbet Farthing — Andrew Corbet was granted a patent to strike farthings in 1693. This was almost immediately revoked, but a few pieces still exist.

Counterfeit — A coin (or note) made outside the relevant issuing authority to cheat someone, although it may well have the same metal content as the original. Interestingly, when the sovereign was demonetised, Italian counterfeiters made sovereigns with slightly more gold than the originals. Because of this they could not be prosecuted and profited from the 44% premium over gold content that sovereigns sold for at the time.

Countermark — A mark or design placed on a coin either by an issuing authority or by a private individual. During the reign of George III a small bust of the king was counterstamped on silver coins to make them legal tender in the United Kingdom. An individual can counterstamp a coin with his or her name or initials. In the 1800s many companies counterstamped advertising slogans on coins to get free advertising. It was later made illegal to deface coins by stamping anything on them.

Cracked Die — When too much pressure is applied when striking coins or when the die is very worn it will start to crack. As the metal is pushed into the die it will also be pushed into the crack, so cracks will appear as raised lines on a coin. It is possible to estimate when during the life of a die the coin was made, by the state and length of the die crack on the coin. A famous example is the Cromwell Crown.

Crosier or crozier — The hook shaped top part of a Bishop's staff, usually found as a mark in legends.

Crown Gold — Henry VIII set the standard for gold to be .916 2/3 fine, known as 22 carat gold. The Mint still uses this standard today.

Glossary

Crown	The first English coin of this denomination was issued by Henry VIII in 1526. It was a gold coin with a face value of four shillings and sixpence. It is very rare because it was shortly replaced with the Crown of the Double Rose, which has a face value of five shillings. The first silver crown was issued in 1551 by Edward VI and the last crown to be issued was in 1981, for the wedding of Prince Charles and Lady Diana Spencer.
Cruciform Shields	Shields in the form of a cross.
Cupro-nickel	An alloy of copper and nickel. Today the usual ratio is 75% copper to 25% nickel.
Currency	From the Latin *currentia*, a stream. Thus anything that flows from one hand to another: coins, banknotes, pigs, shells or any medium of exchange which is acceptable. Today we use the term to refer to paper money.
Cut Money	In the early days when you wanted to pay someone a halfpenny and you only had a silver penny, you literally cut it in half. If you needed farthings then you cut the coin into quarters.
Debasement	When a government uses less precious metal in the coining of money, while still retaining its original face or exchange value. The prime example is the posthumous coinage of Henry VIII which contained so much copper that the thin silver veneer wore off quickly.
Decimalization	In 1971 the British monetary system was finally changed to one based on tens or decimals. The Pounds, Shillings and Pence or 'LSD' system (Libra, Solidus, Denarius) was withdrawn and a new system of 'New Pence' introduced. The pound was no longer divided into twenty shillings or 240d, but into 100p.
Declaration Type	Coins of Charles I issued during the Civil War period, the reverse of which contained the official royalist declaration RELIGO PROTESTANTIUM LEGES ANGLIAE LIBERTAS PARLIAMENTI -The religion of the Protestants the laws of England the liberty of Parliament.
Demonetised	A currency which is deemed to be no longer legal tender for debts both public and private. Under the Currency Reform Act of 1816 all coins issued before that date were demonetised, no longer legal tender. A period of grace was given during which the public could turn their old money in for the new coins. After that period of grace the coins were only worth their metal or intrinsic value.
Denomination	The name given to value of the coin either real or implied. A florin is to the value of two shillings or ten pence.

Coincraft's Coin Checklist

Denticles Design objects used to create a border on a coin, usually round or wedge shaped. They go all around the edge of a coin next to the rim.

Device That part of the design which is not a portrait or lettering.

Die Axis There are two main types of die axis: coin alignment and medal alignment. In coin alignment if you are looking at the 'heads' side and turn the coin over through a vertical axis 180 degrees to the reverse, the reverse will be upside down. If on the other hand the reverse is right side up, then this is medal alignment.

Die Break A raised line which is caused by the metal of the flan being forced into a small crack or break in the die.

Die Numbering on Coins The Royal Mint used to number their dies on some of the silver coins between 1864 and 1879. It was for experimentation, the object of which has been lost. It has been mooted that the Mint was trying to see how long dies lasted.

Die Variety Because different pairs of dies are used to strike similar coins, there may be small differences on the coins. These small differences caused by different dies are called die varieties. As obverse and reverse dies wear out at different times, it is possible to link the dies used by comparing die combinations. Museums spend a lot of time in trying to follow the sequence of dies used and many scholarly papers have been written on the subject.

Die Wear Dies as they strike a vast number of coins start to show signs of wear; this causes the coins they strike to appear rather weakly struck. Coins can be as struck but appear to be only Very Fine.

Die The engraved metal piece which is used to strike coins and medallions. In the old days an engraver cut directly into and in reverse in the metal. Today a plaster is sculptured and a rubber is made which is then placed on a reduction machine. The end product is called a hub and is raised like coins. From this, dies are struck and then hardened before use.

Dorrien Magens Shilling A shilling issued in 1798 by the Royal Mint for the banking firm of Dorrien Magens. The government refused to allow this private enterprise to have its own coinage struck and so had all but about six examples melted down.

Glossary

Double Florin A denomination of four shillings struck only three times in our history. The first was issued in 1887, the Jubilee year of Queen Victoria, and continued on in general circulation until 1890. It is also known as 'the barmaid's ruin'. When she had a few drinks she would often give change for a crown (5/-) instead of a double florin (4/-). This shortage would have to be made up out of her own wages. There were pattern issues in the reigns of George V, George VI and Elizabeth II. All these patterns are rare.

Drapery Clothing or cloth in folds.

Dump Issue A name used for the thick copper farthings and halfpennies of George I in 1717 and 1718.

Durham House This was the Palace of the Bishop of Durham in London, situated along what is now the Strand. It was in operation as a mint in the reign of Edward VI from 1548-1549.

Durham A town where coins were issued over a very long period of time. Regal coinage was issued under William I onwards. Episcopal coinage started under Edward I and continued until the reign of Henry VIII.

E.I.C. The initials of the East India Company, which were used on some gold coins issued from 1729-1739.

Early Soho Striking A contemporary or near contemporary proof struck at the Soho mint, Birmingham, shortly after the dies were cut. See also *Late Soho Striking*.

Early Striking When a new pair of dies is first used they are heavily polished and thus the first few coins struck will have a prooflike appearance. These coins tend to demand a premium price and in many cases are much rarer than proofs.

Edge Inscription Lettering on the edge of a coin which makes up a motto, first used on Cromwell coins. The inscription made it impossible to clip a coin.

Edge Nicks Because of the way coins are struck and then dumped into a bucket or some other receptacle, they fall on top of each other. The edge of the coins can sustain nicks some minute and some substantial. These nicks decrease the value of coins and some dealers will try to put the nick 'right'. Be careful.

Edge Ornament A design on the edge of coin applied using a collar.

Edge Plain Indicates no milling or design on the edge of a coin. Often early proof coins will have a plain edge to differentiate proof coins from circulation strikes.

Coincraft's Coin Checklist

EF (Extremely Fine)	A grade where there is little actual wear except on the high points. On copper and bronze original lustre might well still be in evidence. A most appealing and attractive grade, much undervalued by the market place in its inane seeking of the ultimate perfection.
Effigy	The bust or portrait on the coin or medallion.
Eighteen Pence Token	A silver token coinage issued by the Bank of England to help with a shortage of small change. Issued between 1811 and 1816.
Electrotype	A copy of a coin or medal which has been made by a process of electrolysis. These pieces are made in two parts and then glued or soldered together. They can be very deceptive but if lightly tapped on the rim, electrotypes will not give the characteristic ringing sound of a genuine coin.
Emergency Money	Money which is issued outside the Mint during a time when the normal issuing authority cannot strike coins. It could be because of a siege (Civil War) or a shortage of small coins (Bank of England tokens).
En Medaille	If holding a coin between your fingers with the head side upright, you flip it over 180° through a vertical axis and the reverse side is upright, then this is struck en medaille. If the reverse is upside down then this is struck in coin rotation.
Enamelled Coins	In Victorian days fine engravers and jewellers made current and older coins into attractive jewellery by enamelling them. The surface was scraped off and the design re-engraved into the surface which was then filled with enamel. The workmanship ranged from poor to excellent. The latest coins that I have seen properly enamelled where those of Edward VII. The coins that are being sold today as enamelled are just piled high with acrylic paint and fired in a kitchen stove. Collectors will never collect these modern examples which prostitute the craftsmanship of Victorian and Edwardian times.
English Shilling	When George VI came to the throne a Scottish shilling was struck for the first time (1937). To balance this there was also a shilling with English representation. This continued until 1970 when the last shillings were struck.
Engrailing	The term for the type of lines on the edge of a coin.
Engraver's marks	Sometimes die engravers are permitted to put their name or initials on a die, so every coin that is struck from it will bear their name or mark. Under William Wyon there were many varieties of his famous 'WW' engraver's mark on our coinage.

Glossary

Engraver	The person who actually cuts the dies from which coins or medallions will be struck. He engraves into the metal.
Engraving	The action of cutting the dies from which coins are struck.
Error	Something which has gone wrong either in the striking of a coin or the printing of a banknote. Maybe the coin is struck off centre, double struck or struck on the wrong flan. Collectors will pay extra for a major error on a common coin; on a rare coin they will usually pay less.
Escutcheon	Shield bearing a coat of arms.
Essay	A proposed design for a coin which may or may not be accepted.
Exergue	That part of a coin's design which is separated by a line below the base.
F (Fine)	A grade when the coin or note has seen considerable wear, but is still very collectable. Many collectors like a used coin because they feel that it has actually been somewhere. Collectors on a budget also like this grade.
Facing	When the portrait on a coin or medal is head on to the viewer.
Fair	A grade where the coin has seen much wear and it is only just discernible what the coin is. Collectors usually stay away from this grade unless the coin or note is especially rare or expensive.
Fantasy	A coin struck not to copy something else but rather to be something completely new out of someone's imagination. Over the years fantasy coins have the habit of becoming acceptable to collectors. Many have a very low mintage and can be far more attractive than regularly issued coins.
Farthing	The quarter part of a penny which is in turn the 240th part of a pound. The farthing was first introduced in the reign of Henry III and was last struck in 1956. The former was silver and the latter bronze.
FDC	See *Fleur de Coin*
Fiat Money	A medium of exchange where we accept the value that a government or issuing body puts on something. Real money has an intrinsic or metal value, fiat money has the backing in principal of a government.
Field	That part of the coin where there are no portraits or devices.
Fifty Shillings	A rare gold coin of the Commonwealth period with Cromwell's portrait.

Filled Dies	From time to time a die will become filled with lint, grease or something else. When coins are struck from filled dies part of the design will not be struck up at all. A good example is the Gothic Florin whose design was so fine that occasionally parts of the coin would appear changed and this caused havoc in the roman numeral dates of this series.
Filler	A coin in poor condition bought by a collector until a better example is found.
Fillet	A head band; often used in describing Victoria's portraits which have either a plain or an ornamented fillet.
Find	The locating of a group of coins and or artefacts which have been buried or hidden. Two examples of famous finds are the two Colchester Hoards of Henry III pennies and the Reigate Hoard of Henry VI coins.
Fine Work	William III's gold coinage of 1701 where the workmanship is of especially good quality.
Fishtail Lettering	Style of lettering where the end of the letters resembles a fish tail, only used on the coinage of Richard II.
Flan	The piece of metal upon which the design of the coin will be struck, also called a planchet or blank.
Fleur de Coin	A French term which translates as 'flower of the die' and means Uncirculated. This term was used far more when coins were either mint or used. Today we use the term to represent a full mint state coin in impeccable condition (perfect Uncirculated of at least choice quality). Used far more on the Continent than in Great Britain today.
Florin	Originally a gold and a silver coin issued in Florence, Italy in 1252. First struck here in 1344 and then abandoned until 500 years later. Issued by Victoria as the first attempt at decimalization in 1849. Equivalent to two shillings or the tenth part of a pound, today it is ten pence.
Forgery	A copy of a coin or note made to deceive when exchanged for goods or services. In the old days you were hanged for just possessing a counterfeit, later convicted culprits were transported to Australia. See also *Contemporary Forgery*.
Fourpence	A denomination also called a groat, being one third of a shilling and one sixtieth of a pound. First issued under Edward I.

Glossary

Frosting	Frosting can be the matting of the bust or lettering on a proof coin to show contrast with the brilliant field of the coin. Such a coin is the silver proof 1977 crown, which has almost a 'Wedgwood' effect. Frosting can also be part of the design of a coin such as the William and Mary halfcrown.
G (Good)	A grade which denotes a considerable amount of wear. The coin is discernible but the lettering may not be clearly visible.
Gem Uncirculated	A grade of a coin struck for circulation. I consider this to be the highest grade that a coin can achieve. There must be full and outstanding lustre, an exceptional strike, no nicks and only the smallest bag marks discernible under a strong glass. This quality is harder to achieve in larger sized coins than in smaller sized ones. Fewer than 2% of all Uncirculated coins can be called Gem.
George Noble	A rare denomination issued by Henry VIII, which had Saint George on it.
Ghosting	When dies come together without a flan in between, you may get a partial image of one die on the other. When coins are struck from this die the resulting coins will have one strong image and one weak image of the other die all on one side.
Gilt	Gold plating on either silver or copper. In the reign of George III many of the proof issues were gold plated.
Godless	The first florins issued during the reign of Victoria, in 1849. The legend omitted the phrase DEI GRATIA (by the grace of God) and the issue became known as the Godless Florin. The coins were recalled and a new version was issued in 1851.
Gold	A precious metal and, for most of history, the precious metal **par excellence**.
Gothic Crown	A crown issued in 1847 for circulation with a very ornate design, gothic in nature and thus became known as the Gothic Crown. Patterns were issued of this same design in 1846 and examples dated 1853 were included in the proof set of that year. Considered by many to be the most attractive British coin ever struck. The mintage of the 1847 issue is between 7,000 and 8,000 pieces.
Grade	A verbal, or in the United States, a numerical way of trying to describe the quality of a coin. Because the price of a coin is in many ways dependent on the grade, some individuals will try to overstate the grade of a coin.
Grain	A weight where one grain equals 0.064799 grams.
Graining	The milled edge design of a coin.

Coincraft's Coin Checklist

Great Recoinage — There have been a number of Great Recoinages over the years. There comes a point in time where coins have a problem circulating because they are of different weights and finenesses or have become very worn. Two recoinages which are very important are that of William III in 1696 and that of George III of 1816.

Groat — A coin to the value of fourpence, first issued in the reign of Edward I and struck for use up until the time of Victoria. The coin is struck today for inclusion in the Maundy Set.

Guinea — The denomination of a gold coin which had a face value of twenty-one shillings or £1.05 in new money. It got its name originally because much of the gold used in striking the coins came from Guinea in Africa. First issued under Charles II in 1663.

Half Crown — A denomination made up of two shillings and sixpence. The first silver issue was by Edward VI in 1551; before then it had been a gold coin.

Half Farthing — A denomination used more in the colonies than in this country. Issued by George IV, William IV and Victoria.

Half Groat — Twopence or half of a fourpence groat.

Halfpenny — The half portion of a penny. The first halfpenny was issued by Henry I and the last predecimal coin was struck in 1970.

Hammered — The striking of a coin by placing a flan or blank between two dies and then having someone swing a heavy hammer down on the dies to impress that piece of metal with the image on the dies. The other type of minting is called milled, which is a misnomer. The coins do not have to have milled edges, but rather be struck by machines.

Harp Strings — In the reign of Charles II and some other reigns the number of harp strings on the reverse varied, possibly to indicate which dies were being used.

Harrington — A licence was issued to Lord Harrington to strike farthings by James I. These coins were legal tender.

Hearts — Some George III shillings and sixpences dated 1787 have hearts in one section of the reverse shield and are known as the 'with hearts' variety, others omit them and are known as the 'no hearts' variety.

Heaton Mint — A private mint situated in Birmingham. Famous for the 'H' mintmark and has struck coins for many countries including British pennies in 1912, 1918 and 1919.

Glossary

Hoard — A group of coins which have been buried or hidden by an someone in the past who anticipated coming back to dig them up. Usually, but not always, they are the same generic type of coin.

Holed — or **pierced**. The making of a hole in a coin after it has left the mint. Done to enable the coin to be worn or to demonetise it.

Hub — The positive pair of metal dies from which striking dies can be made. These reversed dies are then used to do the actual striking of the coins.

Imitation Money — Copies of coins made usually as play money rather than to deceive anyone. The most famous of the manufacturers was Lauer of Nuremberg.

Imitation Spade Guinea — A copy in brass of the George III gold guinea known as the spade guinea, because of the appearance of the shield on the reverse. There are many hundreds of different designs. The original pieces were struck by a company called Kettle. A Victorian actress was known to shower the audience with these at the end of her act. They are not valuable but make a wonderful area to attempt to collect.

Incuse — A design which is sunk in rather than raised. Some initials on the coinage of William IV exist with both raised and incused lettering under the bust.

Initial Cross — The cross centred at the top of the coin. The legend will commence at this point.

Intrinsic — The actual metal value of the coin. In the past the intrinsic or metal value was very close to the face value of the coin. It had to be that way otherwise no one would accept the coins in payment. Today we are told that the piece of metal has a face value of £5 and we accept it although the intrinsic value might well be only a few pence. See *fiat money*.

Jeton — These are counters as used from the 12th to the 19th centuries, there are also later pieces which have advertising on them. Derived from the French, it is not a word that is used much in this country today. Jetons were used in mathematical calculations and later in games.

Joey — Slang name for a silver threepence, after Joseph Hume.

Jubilee Coinage	Queen Victoria finally allowed new coins to be issued with a portrait other than her young head. These young head coins were issued from 1838-1887. Her vanity was such that the coins carried her portrait as a 17 year old even when she was 67. On the Jubilee of her reign the new design was struck along with a new denomination (the double florin). The small crown placed on the back of the queen's head made her look a bit foolish and the jubilee head design was changed again in 1893 to the old or widow head coinage.
Key Date	The most difficult to obtain dates in a series. For example the 1952 sixpence and the 1950 and 1951 pennies. These are the dates which you would not find in your change no matter how hard you looked. You would need to go to a dealer and buy them to complete your collection.
Kings Norton Mint	A private mint situated in Birmingham. Known for the 'KN' mintmark. Issued many coins for overseas governments and struck pennies for this country in 1918 and 1919.
Late Soho Striking	Coins struck by the Soho mint some years after the dies were first cut. The coins will normally exhibit defects such as rust marks or die cracks, although usually these flaws are only noticeable on close inspection. In 1848 W.J. Taylor, a contemporary medallist, acquired many of the original dies from which he restruck many of the earlier Soho coins, including patterns, nearly always repolishing or re-engraving some elements of the original die before reusing them.
Laureate	A bust crowned with a wreath of laurel leaves.
Laurel	The James I gold twenty shilling piece first struck in 1619. It gets its 'name' from the laurel wreath on the king's head.
Legend	The inscription found on a coin or medal. In many cases it will consist of a string of abbreviations of Latin words.
Lennox farthings	Farthings struck under the licence that James I gave to Lord Lennox.
Leopard	A rare gold coin issued by Edward III in 1344 with a value of three shillings. The figure shown is actually a lion and not a leopard.
Light Coinage	Weights of coins reduced to make them more in line with the weight of European coins during the reigns of Henry IV and Edward IV.

Glossary

Lima Coinage — Coins issued in 1745 and 1746 by George II from silver captured by Anson from the Spanish. It is thought by some that the silver had originally come from Lima, Peru and it was George II's way of thumbing his nose at the Spanish by placing the name Lima below his bust on the coins.

Lion of Nassau — The lion in the centre of the coins of William III.

Lombardic lettering — Medieval lettering originating in Italy. More rounded and ornamental than the plainer styles that replaced it, it was used until about the time of Edward VI.

Long Cross Coinage — The penny coinage first issued by Henry III where the cross on the reverse came to the outer edge of the coin. It is said that the cross came to the edge for either of two reasons, the first was to help with cutting the coin into halves or quarters and make change. The second was that it hindered the clipping of coins. As both halfpennies and farthings were introduced by Henry III (but are extremely rare), I am more convinced by the second reason!

Love Token — A coin which is engraved with a sentiment, picture or both to show tenderness from one person to another. In Victorian times a young lady might be given any number of engraved threepences or sixpences in this way and it was customary to wear them on a charm bracelet.

Low Relief — Dies which are cut with the design in relief which does not protrude from the surface a great deal.

Low Tide — A variety on the 1902 penny and halfpenny coinage of Edward VII.

Lustre — The brilliant rich colour that coins have when they have just been struck. It is impossible to replace this lustre once it has been lost, but some people will attempt to replace the colour, for profit. There is a certain swirl to the lustre. In copper and bronze coins, the more of the original orange brilliance a coin has, the more desirable it is.

Maltravers farthings — Farthings struck by Lord Maltravers who had been licensed by Charles I.

Matt Proof — A special finish which leaves a dull surface on the coin. This country issued matt proofs only in 1902 as an experiment; it was not repeated.

Coincraft's Coin Checklist

Maundy Money — Associated with the royal ceremony celebrating Maundy Thursday which is believed to go back to the reign of Edward II. The first 'sets' can be made up from the hammered coins of Charles II but no real Maundy sets were made until the end of the reign of George III. A Maundy set consists of one of each of the denominations of fourpence, threepence, twopence and penny; mintages are low. Recipients of Maundy money get one penny for every year that the reigning monarch has been alive. So when Elizabeth II was 60, each person got 60 pence (six sets of four coins). When she was 61, they got six sets plus a 1 penny piece. When she was 62 they got six sets plus a 2 pence and so on.

Medal — An award usually given for valour and intended to be worn. Given by the government or some official organisation.

Medalet — A small sized medallion.

Medallion — A commemorative piece struck to honour an individual, event, place, time or the like. May or may not be issued by a government. If the event is of importance, many different companies may issue many different pieces.

Mestrelle or Meystrell — A French engraver who introduced the method of striking coins that we call today 'milled coinage'. Elizabeth I experimented with coins struck on a screw press between 1561 and 1571. Very neat workmanship and of a vastly superior quality than hammered coins. But the Mint employees feared that this new machinery would put them out of a job and Mestrelle was dismissed. In 1578 he was hung for counterfeiting!

Metal Transfer — During striking, metal flows from one side of the coin to the other to fill the die. A vague outline can be seen on the 'wrong' side of the coin. Not to be confused with clashed dies.

Military Guinea — The last gold guinea ever to be struck was dated 1813. It is called the Military Guinea not because of the design but because it was struck for paying troops rather than for general circulation.

Milled — A misnomer for machine struck coinage. Originally, one of the most important features of machine struck coins was that they could have their edge milled to prevent clipping. Milling was later replaced with lettering and then reintroduced. But the generic term milled indicates machine struck.

Milling — The actual lines or grooves around the edge of a coin which can be straight or slanting.

Glossary

Mint abbreviation — On the early hammered coins the moneyer's name was spelled out in full but, due to lack of space on the reverse of a coin, the name of the mint might have to be abbreviated.

Mint Set — A set of uncirculated coins specially issued by a mint. The coins will usually have a special packaging and/or quality of the surfaces to distinguish them from regular circulation issues. The Royal Mint first issued Mint Sets in 1982 and have done so every year since.

Mint Sport — A coin struck illicitly but from genuine dies to produce an error or novelty of some kind.

Mint — As a grading term it is the same as Uncirculated, indicating a coin which has not seen circulation. Mint of course also refers to a place where coins are struck.

Mintage — The number of coins of an issue that were struck.

Mintmark — Also known as 'privy mark'. A symbol or mark placed on a coin to differentiate it from other similar coins struck elsewhere and indicate where and by whom it had been struck. Used to control the quality of the coins being struck, these marks substituted the practice of including the moneyer's name in the legend. If something was wrong with the weight or the metal content of the coins, then the monarch knew who to 'speak to'. A mintmark was used for some hammered issues and on milled issues. It could help link dies to coins and sometimes undated coins can be dated accurately by their mintmark.

Mirror Finish — When the surface of the planchet or flan has the appearance of brightness without flaws. This surface is found on proof coins where both the flan and the dies are polished to achieve perfection.

Misstrike — A coin which in any of a number of ways is not struck correctly. It might be off centre, it might be double struck or it might even be a brockage.

Model Coins — The model penny was struck by Joseph Moore of Birmingham ca 1844. It was a copper outer ring with a silvered inner part. It caused confusion with the public and the Mint had to tell the public that it was not legal tender. Other coins struck in much smaller size are usually by Lauer of Nuremberg; these were used as play money for children.

Modified Effigy — Refers to a change in the design of the coinage of George V in 1926.

Coincraft's Coin Checklist

Moneyer — During the hammered coinage, a moneyer was the mint official responsible for the striking of the coins and ensuring they were of the legal weight and metal fineness. On late Anglo-Saxon and early post-Conquest coins, his name will appear on the reverse together with the name of the mint.

Mounting — A coin can be mounted in either of two ways. The first is by attaching a loop to the coin with solder. The second is by constructing a ring or bezel to fit around the coin and placing a chain through a ring in the bezel. Both will decrease the value of a coin; one rapidly, the other slowly.

Mule — If you take one die from one coin and another die from a second coin and combine the two dies to make a third coin, this third coin is called a mule. When Taylor had the Soho Mint dies, he muled many different coins to come up with an equal number of new varieties.

NCLT — See *Non Circulating Legal Tender*

'New' Coins — An indication on the decimal coinage from 1968 to 1981 to show that these were New Pence, not old pence.

New Style Calendar — In 1752 the calendar changed from Julian to Gregorian.

Newark — A town in the Midlands which during the Civil War was surrounded and held to siege. Emergency coinage was 'struck' from cut up pieces of silver dinner plates. As some of the plates were gold plated silver so are the coins. They are dated 1645 and 1646 and the denominations are halfcrown, shilling, 9 pence and 6 pence.

No Hearts — In the 1787 shillings and sixpences there are varieties with hearts in one of the quarters and another variety without hearts; this is known as the no hearts type.

Noble — First struck in 1344 in the reign of Edward III, a gold coin to the value of six shillings and eight pence.

Non Circulating Legal Tender — NCLT coins are the subject of much heated debate in the coin industry. Basically these are most of the commemorative and off metal strikes issued by the mints. They are made for collectors and to gain money for the issuing authority. But if you wanted to spend them in theory you could, thus they are legal tender.

Northumberland Shilling — George III had struck £100 (2,000 pieces) of a special shilling in 1763. It was to be used by the Duke of Northumberland for largesse when he entered Dublin as the Lord Lieutenant of Ireland. It has a distinct bust.

Glossary

Notaphily — The collecting of banknotes or financial instruments made of paper.

Numismatics — The study of coins, medals, tokens, banknotes and other means of exchange. Such a broad field encompasses a very wide range of interests, from the historical developments associated with coins and banknotes or the technical aspects of production to the artistic aspect of the designs -to name but a few.

Obsidional Currency — From the Latin **obsidere**, to besiege, and indicating coins struck at a place that is besieged. In this country the term refers to the issues of the Civil War and encompasses Carlisle, Colchester, Newark, Pontefract and Scarborough. These issues are crude, being struck under extreme outside pressures and usually from cut up silverware.

Obverse — The side of a coin which bears the monarch's portrait or the most important legend, which usually includes the name of the monarch or the country. This is considered the most important side of the coin and commonly known as 'heads'.

Off Metal Strike — Sometimes a flan for one coin will accidentally be struck with the dies of another denomination. If these coins are issued in two different metals then the resulting coin will be known as an off metal striking. Today mints offer their coinage in both the original metal and in silver and gold strikings; there is confusion as to what to call these.

Off-centre — A coin which is imperfectly struck so that part of the design is missing, as a result of careless minting procedures. In the case of hammered coins, such as those of Henry I and Stephen, they were met with very frequently. Off-centred coins are generally of less value than well-centred ones, even when the condition is otherwise excellent.

Old Head — The last coinage of Queen Victoria which is also known as the widow head coins. She is portrayed wearing the veil of widowhood.

One Year Type — A major variety which is only struck and issued for one year. Examples are the George IV 1821 shilling and 1849 florin of Victoria.

Ornamental Trident — On the copper pennies of Victoria, Britannia is holding a trident; this comes both plain and ornamented.

Overdate	When dies have to be reused at a later date, rather than engrave new ones, a new date or part thereof is punched over the existing date. The overdate can only really be seen properly on high quality coins. In the Commonwealth there are some coins where the date has been repunched two or even three times. This saved the making of new dies, money and time.
Overseas Mints	When English coins were struck at mints other than in Great Britain, such as Calais during the reign of Henry VI.
Overstrike	When a coin is struck over an already existing coin. Examples are the Bank of England Dollar which was overstruck on Spanish eight reales.
Oxford Crown	A now very rare silver crown issued for the City of Oxford during the Civil War. It is dated 1644, was designed by Thomas Rawlins and shows the City of Oxford below the king on horseback.
Parliament, Tower Mint under	During the Civil War in the reign of Charles I, the Tower Mint fell under the control of Parliament and coins with the portrait of Charles I were struck.
Patina or Patination	The toning that a coin has built up over a number of years. Many collectors, especially those just starting out, do not like what they call 'dirty' coins. I believe that nice patination not only enhances the appearance of coins but actually increases their value. Patina is something which comes naturally and cannot be reproduced artificially.
Pattern	A proposed design for a new coin. When a new coin is going to be issued a number of engravers will be asked to submit their designs, before the final design is chosen. Once the actual design is chosen a number of examples will be struck before the date of issue for circulation. Even though these have the same appearance as the coin to be struck, because of the date they are considered to be patterns. An example is the 1848 florin of Victoria which is the same design as the issued 1849 coin.
Pax	The word for Peace which appears on the pennies of William I and Henry I. It was a hope for peace in the country.
Peck, C. Wilson	The author of the standard work on the copper and bronze coins of England.
Penny	The denomination is from Denarius a Roman coin, which then became a denier in Europe and penny here which is abbreviated as 'd'.

Glossary

Petition Crown Thomas Simon submitted the design for a crown to Charles II in 1663. The workmanship was excellent and Simon managed to get two lines of text on the edge of the coin. He petitioned the king to accept his designs but was turned down, reportedly because the king could not forgive him for the coins he had engraved in Cromwell's time.

Piedfort A French word for a coin which is thicker than the usual striking. There can be double, triple and six times thickness piedforts. In 1983 the Royal Mint started to issue special collectors examples of the new pound coin in silver proof piedfort and it proved to be very popular.

Pile The lower die in the pair of dies used to strike hammered coins. It usually had a sharp pointed end which could be stuck into the wood to hold it in place.

Pinches Family A family of medallists who became the engravers in the mid 1800s. Engraved coins and medallions and did some outstanding work.

Pingo, Lewis (1743-1830) Assistant engraver at the Royal Mint from 1776 and chief engraver from 1779-1815. Engraved many coins and patterns.

Pinhole On the edge of coins you will sometimes see two pin holes; these were made to hold the coin in a mount as jewellery.

Pistrucci, Benedetto (1784-1855) Engraver of gems as well as of the St George and the dragon reverse still used on coins today. The design was originally used on the 'new' sovereign of George III, struck in 1817.

Pitting Small holes in the surface of a coin or die caused by oxidation. If the die is pitted, then the coins it is used to strike will have small raised bumps on their surfaces. Many restrike coins can be told from the originals by the pitting or lack of it.

Plain Edge Proof Proofs of George III, William IV and Victoria often have plain edges to differentiate them from circulating coins.

Planchet The flan or blank that is used to strike coins.

Plaster A sculptor will use a round piece of plaster to engrave his design. From this plaster a rubber will be made. The rubber will be placed on a reduction machine to make hubs from which a die is made. The plaster will be much larger than the finished coin; this is to enable the fineness of the design to be engraved without the use of magnifying glass.

Plug	Some coins have a plug in them to prevent counterfeiting such as the tin coins of James II. When a coin has been holed after striking, a plug may be placed in the hole to make the coin look more attractive.
Pontefract	A Royalist stronghold in the Civil War, under siege from June 1648 until March 1649. Emergency moneys were issued struck from silver dinner plates.
Portcullis Coinage	These were coins issued by Elizabeth I for use overseas by the East India Company in 1600-1601. They were trade coins and were struck with the denominations of 8, 4, 2 and 1 terstern and weighed the same as 8, 4, 2, and 1 reale respectively. They get their name by the depiction of a portcullis or drop gate on them.
Post-Union	After the Union of England and Scotland in 1707.
Posthumous issue	Coins of a monarch struck after his/her death.
Pre-Union	Before the Union of England and Scotland in 1707.
Presentation Piece	A coin specially struck to be given to a very important person. Sometimes the coin will be struck to a higher than normal quality, sometimes it will be struck in a more precious metal and sometimes it will be struck with a commemorative reverse. Presentation pieces were often made to show a monarch the new coinage or new designs.
Prince Elector Guinea	The guinea of George I issued in 1714 where the legend reads PR EL in place of EL; it also has a very different head.
Privy mark	See *Mintmark*.
Proof Set	A set of coins issued in proof quality by a mint. The coins will, in modern times, come in a case or some sort of presentation packaging.
Proof	In this country proof is a method of striking and not a condition. A proof coin is struck most carefully with polished dies and a polished flan. It will be struck more than once to get the high relief to show all the fine details. Sometimes you will get a lead piece with half of a coin, this is done to proof the die before striking.
Prooflike	A condition when the coins are issued in a quality which is better than the normal circulation striking but not up to Proof quality. The surfaces will shimmer.

Glossary

Provenance mark	A symbol or mark on a coin to identify the origin of the metal it was struck on. Thus plumes, for example, indicate Welsh silver or silver from the Welsh Copper Co; roses, the mines in the West of England; VIGO, silver captured at the battle of Vigo in 1702.
Provincial Mints	The Great Recoinage of 1696 caused so much work that provincial mints had to be opened again. They were Bristol, Chester, Exeter, Norwich and York.
Pseudo Coin	A fantasy which purports to be a coin when it is usually a medallic piece.
Punch or Puncheon	A design or lettering on a piece of metal which is then applied to make a portion of a die. The head of George III might be made as a punch so that every die made for that coin will have the same details. It could be for applying lettering or a mintmark.
Pyx, Trial of the	From the Greek *pyxis*, a box or vase. The Trial of the Pyx is the testing of the quality of the metal of coins by placing them in boxes at the Goldsmith's Hall, picking samples at random and assaying them to test the purity of the metal.
Quarter Farthing	The smallest denomination ever struck in this country. There were 3,840 of these coins to the pound. They were issued by Victoria and struck in copper; they are scarce.
Quarter Guinea	A gold coin with a face value of five shillings and three pence. Only issued by George I in 1718 and George III in 1762.
Quatrefoil	Four pellets close together.
Raised Edge Proof	On the 1935 George V crown the lettering on the edge of the coin was raised to differentiate it from the incuse lettering on the circulation strikes.
Rarity	An attempt to describe how many examples of a coin still exist. When an exact number are not known then a scale of rarity is used. A scale might go from EC (Extremely Common) to S (Scarce), or from R for Rare to R5 for Extremely Rare. This 'guesstimate' of the number available is usually based on knowledge rather than mint reports of the number struck.
Rawlins, Thomas	Charles I's chief coin and medal engraver during the Civil War. He worked at Oxford and engraved the beautiful Oxford Crown.
Re-issue	When a mint strikes more coins than was originally planned. It should be in the same year or they then become restrikes. An example is the 1965 Canadian Mint Set. The Canadian Mint had so many orders that it reopened the ordering and struck as many sets as they had call for.

Coincraft's Coin Checklist

Recoinage	When old coins are called in because they are no longer legal tender, melted down and then the metal is made into other coins. The last great recoinages were those of William III and George III.
Reddite Crown	A pattern crown by Thomas Simon for Charles II.
Reducing Machine & Reduction Process	Today when a coin is to be struck, an engraver carves his design in plaster. This plaster is used to make a metal or rubber master which is then placed on a reducing machine. This cuts an exact copy but in a size which is the same as the coin which is to be struck.
Reeding	The milling on the edge of a coin.
Regnal Date	The year on the edge of a coin which is taken from the date of the death of the proceeding monarch. As this may occur in the middle of the calendar year, a single year's coins will often carry two different regnal years during their striking. On the coinage of Charles II, this dates from the death of Charles I, 30 January 1649.
Relief	The raised portion of the coin design.
Restrike	When coins are struck from the original dies at a later time. Many of the coins from the Soho Mint were restruck when Taylor bought the old dies for scrap metal value. Until the 1960s the Indian government would strike coins going back to the period of Victoria for you if you gave them old rupees in their place. Collectors should be aware that restrikes exist and that they do not bring as much as the original strikes do. Restrikes also diminish the value of the original strikings.
Reverse	The 'tails' side of the coin, the opposite of the obverse or 'heads' side.
Ribbon Stain	In 1950 and 1951 proof sets the chemicals in the ribbon interact with the coins and often result in stains on the coins which cannot be removed.
Richmond Farthings	The Duchess of Richmond was licensed to issue farthings by Charles I.
Rim	The raised part of a coin, formed by the metal from the edge being extruded.
Rose Ryal	A gold coin issued by James I. The king is sitting on his throne and the reverse has the Tudor Rose.

Glossary

Rust Marks — Unless carefully kept, dies will rust. Coins struck from rusted dies will show areas of pitting. It is more commonly found on hammered than milled coins, though some Soho Mint proof and pattern coins struck at a later date also show rust marks.

Ryal — Edward IV first struck this gold coin in 1465; it had a value of ten shillings.

Scarborough — A town which, when it was besieged during the Civil War, issued many different denominations, all cut from silver dinner plates. There are many known denominations and all are rare. Rather than try to have uniform denominations they cut the silver, weighed it and then stamped it with its value.

Scottish Shilling — A variety of shilling issued from 1937 to 1970 (see also *English Shilling*).

Scratches — Marks which are incused in the field of a coin. These may have been caused by any number of things. They detract from the appearance and value of a coin.

Seignorage — The difference between the metal or intrinsic value of the planchet plus the cost of striking deducted from the face value of the coin. In the past this was a relatively small proportion of the value, today it is increasingly larger. It is interesting to note that some small denominations actually cost more to strike than their face value.

Shield Reverse — This refers in particular to the first type of Victorian sovereign which had a shield or coat of arms on the reverse of the coin.

Shilling — The first attempt at a shilling which was the twentieth part of a pound, was the Testoon of Henry VII introduced in 1504. The first actual shilling was issued by Edward VI. This is also the first dated English coin; the date was in Roman numerals.

Short Cross Coinage — The penny coinage where the cross on the reverse fell well short of the edge of the coin, issued by Henry II, Richard I, John and Henry III. Henry III had both short and long cross coinage.

Shrewsbury — The first Civil War mint to be opened to strike coinage for Charles I. Thomas Bushell was the mintmaster and took his privy mark of the Welsh plumes with him.

Siege Money — Money issued by a locality under siege when the normal flow of money into and out of the location is impeded and inhabitants create their own form of exchange or money to service their economic transactions.

Coincraft's Coin Checklist

Silver Tokens	Privately issued silver pieces struck around 1811 to alleviate the shortage of small change. Eventually the Bank of England also issued silver tokens, at which point the private issue ceased.
Sixpence	A denomination of half a shilling containing the value of six one penny coins; there are Victorian patterns with the denomination of half a shilling. The sixpence was first struck in 1551 for the currency reform of Edward VI. It continued to be struck until 1970 and was legal tender till 1980.
Snick	Small piece of metal, usually 'V' shaped, taken out of hammered coins to check their metal content.
Soho Mint	Matthew Boulton's minting facilities in Birmingham, 1786-1809. Among the coins struck there, under contract for the British government, was the famous Cartwheel Twopence.
South Sea Company	The South Sea Company had special coins struck for them in 1723 under George I. The coins were silver issues of sixpence, shilling, halfcrown and crown. They can be distinguished by the letters SSC in the angles between the arms on the reverse.
Sovereign	A gold coin first struck by Henry VII in 1489, to the value of twenty shillings. In 1816 under the Currency Reform Act the guinea was abolished and the sovereign made the unit of gold currency.
Spade Guinea	A gold coin to the value of 21 shillings issued by George III. The shield on the reverse looks like the metal part of a garden spade and thus it acquired the nickname Spade Guinea.
Specimen Set	A set of coins struck for presentation purposes.
Specimen	A specially struck coin for presentation purposes. The surface is usually prooflike.
Spur Ryal	James I gold coin issued in 1604 with a face value of fifteen shillings. The sharp rays of the sun on the reverse look like a spur.
SSC	See *South Sea Company*.
Sterling	When it refers to the fineness of silver it is the British standard of 925 parts silver per 1,000 parts total. British coins were struck in Sterling Silver until 1919, at which point the metal content was changed to 500 fine silver.
Striation	Marks on the coin usually from the scraping off of the excess metal of a coin. Sometimes from an improperly manufactured flan.

Glossary

Tanner, John	Engraver of coins during the reign of George II and George III. A German who came to England in 1728 and died here in 1775, he was responsible for most of George II's coinage.
Tanner	Slang name for a sixpence.
Taylor, William Joseph	(1802-1885) A medallist and die sinker who produced a number of coins and tokens, mainly for export. He is most famous for restriking of coins from the Soho Mint's dies.
Testoon	The forerunner of the shilling issued by Henry VII in 1504 and valued at twelve pence. It weighed 144 grains, twelve times the weight of a penny. A rare coin with his portrait and of artistic importance.
Third Farthing	A coin with the value of one third of a farthing, which in turn is a quarter of a penny which is again one 240th of a pound. Used in some of the colonies.
Third Guinea	A gold coin with the value of seven shillings (35p), three of which made up a guinea, only issued by George III.
Three Farthings	A silver coin to the value of three quarters of a penny, struck only in the reign of Elizabeth I.
Three Halfpence	A coin to the value of one penny and a half issued by Elizabeth I and again by William IV and Victoria, when it was used in overseas colonies, Ceylon, Jamaica and British Guiana.
Three Shilling Token	Bank token, struck in silver and issued by the Bank of England from 1811 until 1816. There are two busts of George III, the first in Roman armour and the second with a laurel wreath.
Threepence	A coin to the value of three pennies.
Tie	The bit on the bottom of the ribbon at the back of the head. Undergoes much change over the issues.
Token	A privately issued piece which stands in for a regal coin of a stated value. Many times the token will have an advertisement for the merchant who issued it. These pieces have less metal and cost less to strike than their purported face value. When there is a shortage of small change these pieces become more readily acceptable by the general populace. The vast influx of issues was in the 17th Century and then again in the late 18th Century. At the end, tokens were being issued for collectors rather than to fill a need in the community.

Coincraft's Coin Checklist

Toning A coin over a period of time will react to its environment. The metal in a coin will change colour many times to a magnificent series of hues, and this is what we call toning. A toned coin is in fact more desirable than an untoned coin and in many cases will bring more money from a collector.

Tooling The enhancement of a coin by burnishing the fields and getting the design to stand out more. It can also be to alter a coin's value by changing the date or some other part of the coin.

Touch Piece When monarchs were held to rule by divine right, it was believed that the process of touching them with a coin and then wearing it constituted a cure for prevalent ailments. A 'Touching Ceremony' first took place in the reign of Edward the Confessor and last in the reign of Queen Anne, and special gold medalets were struck with which to 'touch' the monarch.

Tournai French town were Henry VIII struck coins.

Tower Mint The principal mint of England from Norman days, it was situated in and around the Tower of London. It was actually inside the Tower of London until the early 19th Century.

Triple Unite Issued in the Civil War it is physically the largest gold coin ever struck and had a face value of sixty shillings. It was struck at Shrewsbury and Oxford from 1642 -1644.

Troy Weight A measure of weight for precious metals. Where an ounce of feathers is weighed avoirdupois at 28 grams an ounce of gold is weighed in troy weight at 31.1 grams.

Truncation The bottom part of a bust or neck on a coin, often where the engraver signs his name.

Type Coin A coin which represents a major variety of a coinage rather than a specific date. Collectors often try and obtain one example of each major type rather than one of each date of coin issued.

Type Set A collection of coins put together which shows the different major varieties of the coinage rather than all the dates.

Type A major variety of a coinage such as Victorian crowns can be broken up into four different types: Young Head, Gothic, Jubilee Head and Old Head. A collector would attempt to gather one of each type of crown rather than to complete a date set of Victorian crowns.

Una and the Lion The design on the Victoria gold £5 issued in 1839.

Glossary

Unc (Uncirculated)	A grade which indicates that a coin has never been released into circulation. Although a coin may be less than perfect when struck, with scratches and nicks, that does not mean that it is not Uncirculated. Over the years a coin may tone or a copper coin may change from bright to dark, again this does not mean that it is not Uncirculated. The term literally means a coin which has not seen circulation.
Uniface	Having a design on one side only.
Unite	A gold coin of James I, first issued in 1604 and with a face value of twenty shillings.
Unpublished Variety	An example with a difference, i.e. lettering differential, metal content, overdate or unknown date which has never been listed in numismatic writings or in a journal.
V.I.P. Proof	A term sometimes used to describe proof coins struck in very small numbers for presentation.
VF (Very Fine)	A grade of coin where there has been obvious but relatively restricted wear on the highest portions of the coin.
VG (Very Good)	A grade where the coin has experienced a lot of wear and where the details are still discernible but worn.
Vigo Coinage	The coinage of Queen Anne struck from silver and gold captured from the Spanish in the battle of Vigo.
WCC	See *Welsh Copper Company*
Weak Strike	When not enough pressure is used to strike the coin, the design will appear to be weak and an Uncirculated coin will look like a used example.
Welsh Copper Company	Shillings were struck under George I with silver which came from the Welsh Copper Company. To distinguish these coins from the normal ones a small 'WCC' is under George's bust. These coins are all scarce and in higher grades are Rare.
Wire Money	Maundy money issued in 1792 by George III, where the shape of the numerals looked like a piece of wire. A one year type.
Wolsey	Cardinal Wolsey had a mint at York from 1514-1526 and struck coins with his initials 'T. W.' on them. He struck a groat which caused problems and a trial. The king was incensed that he dared to strike groats and also that he had placed his initials on the coins.

Wreath Crown	A series of crowns issued from 1927 to 1936 excluding 1935, with a wreath on the reverse. This was the fourth coinage under George V; a proof set was issued in 1927 containing this coin. Mintages are low and it is also known as the Christmas Crown as it was given out as presents at that time of year.
Year Set	A collection or set of coins containing all the coins that were issued in a specific year.
Yeo, Richard	Engraver at the Royal Mint from about 1749. He produced the Northumberland Shilling and guineas of George III and died in 1779.
York	At this town there was an Episcopal mint from about 750 AD and it remained until Archbishop Wolsey struck groats bearing his own initials and the king closed him down. The city was also the location of a mint during the English Civil War and later during the Great Recoinage of 1696-97. The inscription on coins struck in York is EBOR.
Young Head	This has been used for the coinage of George II, George III and Victoria and helps to differentiate the first coins issued during a long reign.

Richard Lobel

Gem English Coinage 1660-1947

Gem French Coinage 1646-1946

United States
Colonial to 1945
RARE DATES   ALL GRADES
AND U.S. GOLD

BUYING
$10 TO $100,000
TYPE COINAGE AND
PAPER MONEY

English Crown, George V

U.S. Morgan $

BUYING SELLING TRADING

French 5 Franc

French 5 Franc

The largest Gem English and Gem French inventory
available every day in the United States. Ungraded and Graded coins.

PCGS AND NGC AVAILABLE

SELLING: send or fax us your want list –
if we can not find it, it is not for sale!!

BUYING: we are in London and Paris every month.
We will be glad to arrange meetings in either city.

American Heritage Minting Inc.

WILLIAM P. PAUL
Benjamin Fox Pavilion
Suite 510, Box 1008
Jenkintown, PA 19046
Tel: 215 576 7272
Fax: 215 576 5915

DAVID NEITA
8306 Wilshire Blvd
Suite 2657, Beverly Hills, Cal 90211
Tel: 213 782 9660
Tel: 213 782 9668
Fax: 213 651 0178

14 Rue Anstile
Poteaux, France
92800

See us on the Internet at ahm.coin.com

COIN
Capsules Trays Cases Albums Accessories

CLASSIC
3-ring padded binder of PVC and 5x20 pocket pages with
white card interleaving............................ (GB p&p £4.50) **8.98**
Spare pages: 20, 30 or 63 pockets each ....**.38**
White card dividers, per 10 ....**1.00**

COINDEX
Coin album with 3-ring padded binder and 8 x 16 pocket pages,
white card interleaving and index cards. Each pocket has a flap
to stop coins from falling out .... (GB p&p £4.50)......................**15.33**
Coindex leaves each..**1.02**
Dividers each ....**.26**
100 envelopes and cards **6.13**

The coin collecting storage system. Free of chlorine and acids, these drawers contain no sulphur compounds to discolour the coins or medals. Outside dimensions 294mm x 236mm x 303mm. Drawers can be interlocked to form a free-standing unit, whilst still having free movement of the individual drawers. **Each drawer £13.95.**
(GB p&p One Drawer £3.00, 2 or more £4.50)
With square inserts:
2199 for 90 coins up to 19mm dia.
2180 for 80 coins up to 24mm dia.
2149 for 48 coins up to 28mm dia.
2148 for 48 coins up to 30mm dia.
2135 for 35 coins up to 36mm dia.
2115 for 30 coins up to 38mm dia.
2124 for 24 coins up to 42mm dia.
2120 for 20 coins up to 47mm dia.
2145 for 45 assorted coins.

ROUND INSERTS AVAILABLE REFER TO BROCHURE

FULL PRICE LIST AVAILABLE ON REQUEST

Overseas postage at rates prevailing at time of despatch

VERA TRINDER LTD
(INCORPORATING HARRIS PUBLICATIONS) Co.Reg. No. 960117

SHOP OPEN MONDAY-FRIDAY 8.30-5.30 TEL: 0207 836 2365/6
38 BEDFORD STREET, STRAND, LONDON WC2E 9EU

FOR THE LATEST NEWS OF METAL DETECTING FINDS OF COINS AND SPECTACULAR COIN HOARDS

Take out a subscription to

THE SEARCHER
the top magazine for the world's most fascinating hobby

Send for a sample copy to:
Searcher Publications, PO Box 4490,
Long Melford, Suffolk CO10 9SW
Tel: 01787 377711

The Ecu Mint Set

This beautiful seven piece Mint Set contains the 1992 United Kingdom Ecus. Each collection comes in a full colour package, which gives you information about the pieces while keeping them safe.

Each Mint Set contains the 1/10th Ecu, 1/4 Ecu, 1/2 Ecu, 1, 2, 5 and 10 Ecus. The Crown sized 5 Ecu takes pride of place in the centre of the collection. With full colour packaging these make excellent gifts for collectors both in this country and overseas.

You get the whole seven piece collection in the full colour packaging for only £18.95
or order three for only £52.50. You will want one for yourself and your friends.

LEU9205	Ecu Mint Set in Full Colour Package..	£18.95
LEU9290	3 Ecu Mint Sets in Full Colour Packages....................................	£52.50

For the Ecu Mint Set, order by post or telephone quoting CSC040900 and the individual order codes above. Please add £1.95 per order for handling. Allow 14 days for delivery.

We accept Mastercard, Visa, Diners and American Express (quote card number and expiry date).

Send your order to Coincraft Customer Services at –

COINCRAFT
44 & 45 Great Russell Street, London WC1B 3LU
Tel: 0207-636 1188 Fax: 0207-637 7635
Email: info@coincraft.com

COIN NEWS...
....what more do you need?

Phone our credit card hotline on 01404 44166, e-mail us on info@coin-news.com
or visit our website www.coin-news.com

ANCIENT * HAMMERED * MILLED * MODERN
TOKENS * MEDALLIONS * BANK NOTES

All you need to know about coins and coin collecting in one publication.
With informative articles, news, views, market movements,
auction reports and much more.

**COIN NEWS is BRITAIN'S BIGGEST SELLING AND BEST VALUE
coin magazine. Available from all good newsagents or on subscription
direct from the publishers (for rates see below).**

*If you are not familiar with COIN NEWS we are more than happy to send you a free sample on request.
Just phone quoting reference CSC/2000 or fill in the form below*

To: TOKEN PUBLISHING LTD., 1 ORCHARD HOUSE, DUCHY ROAD, HEATHPARK,
HONITON, DEVON, UK EX14 8YD
TEL: 01404 46972   FAX: 01404 831 895
e-mail info@coin-news.com

NAME ....
ADDRESS ....

☐ **Free Sample copy**
or annual subscription rates are as follows:
☐ £28.00 UK/BFPO
☐ £36.00 Europe/World—surface mail
☐ £45.00 World—airmail

*Please make cheques payable to
"Token Publishing Ltd." US Dollar cheques also acceptable*
Credit Card (Visa/Mastercard)

POSTCODE ....
I enclose remittance of £ ....

Although we will not pass your details on to anyone else we may from time to
time send you mailings that we think would be of interest to you,
please tick if you do not require such information ☐

Expiry date ....Signature CSC/2000

WE'RE IN THE HEART OF DOWNTOWN BOSTON.
YOU MAY HAVE NEVER POPPED INTO OUR SHOP...

We are
Boston's Oldest Coin Shop
(Boston, Massachusetts, USA, that is).

BUYING & SELLING
United States, Colonial & Ancient Coins;
Banknotes; Gold & Silver Bullion.

J.J. Teaparty Inc.
49 Bromfield Street
Boston, Mass. 02108-4110
Tel: 001~617~482~2398 ❖ Fax: 001~617~542~0023
e-mail: JJTeaparty@aol.com

PLEASE, VISIT OUR SHOP
IN HISTORICAL DOWNTOWN BOSTON,
YOU WILL BE GLAD YOU DID!

Wynyard Coin Centre
Sydney's Best Known Coin Shop

A nice display of British, Australian, world coins and banknotes for sale. We also buy coins and banknotes.

Visit our shop off George Street for a good selection and friendly service.

M.R. 'Bob' Roberts
Wynyard Coin Centre
7 Hunter Arcade, George Street,
Sydney, N.S.W. Australia.

Tel: 00612-9299-2047
Fax: 00612-9290-3710

Send for a sample copy of
Numi$News®
our FREE list

---

collectable coins and currency

CURRENCY NOTES AND COINAGE AVAILABLE

Jersey is very proud of its independence, being a "Peculiar of the Crown" and, as a direct result, has for many years issued its own currency notes and coinage which carry the sovereign's portrait.
Mail Order accepted, with cash, cheque or Visa card number.

The States Treasury
Cyril Le Marquand House,
St. Helier,
Jersey.

Telephone: 01534 603251
Facsimile: 01534 603256

K.B. COINS

Dealers in ENGLISH COINS—CROWNS TO FARTHINGS including PROOF SETS, PATTERNS and DECIMAL COINAGE

★

We issue regular lists of our rapidly changing stock and will gladly service your 'wants' list

Please send 50p in stamps for huge 70-page catalogue

British Coins Urgently Wanted

We purchase single items, collections or accumulations, especially proof sets

K.B. COINS
50 Lingfield Road, Martins Wood, Stevenage, Herts SG1 5SL
Telephone (01438) 312661
Fax (01438) 311990
Callers by appointment only please

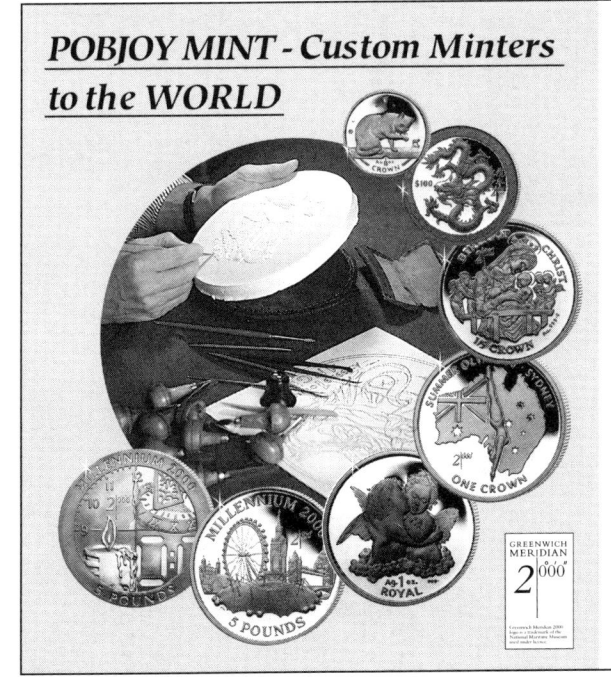

NEW LIST NOW AVAILABLE

BNTA

POBJOY MINT - Custom Minters to the WORLD

Custom Minters to the world, Pobjoy Mint continues to strive to serve governments worldwide producing currency, commemorative and bullion Coins in all types of precious metals and sizes ranging as large as 2 kilos and as small as a 1 gram piece. Consistent winners of top inter-national awards for numismatic excellence, and 5 awards for the Isle of Man alone making their coinage some of the most sought after and unique in the world.

Pobjoy Mint has maintained an impeccable reputation for the crafting of fine objects in precious metals. Now at the turn of the millennium, Pobjoy is firmly established as Europe's premier private mint, having gained worldwide fame for the quality and beauty of its commemorative issues. Pobjoy Mint is also renowned for it's striking of contract jobs and advice to countries on how to go forward with their coinage in the third Millennium.
For more information, please contact Pobjoy Mint direct:
Tel: +44 1737 818181.

Pobjoy Mint Ltd®

Millennia House Kingswood Park Bonsor Drive Kingswood Surrey KT20 6AY England.
Internet: www.pobjoy.com
E-mail: mint@pobjoy.com
Tel: +44 1737 818181
Fax: +44 1737 818199

GRANTA COINS
STAMPS & ANTIQUITIES
23 MAGDALENE STREET
CAMBRIDGE CB3 0AF
TEL/FAX: (01223) 361662
MOBILE: 0831 719313
E.MAIL: coingranta@aol.com

Coins ♦ Stamps ♦ Artefacts ♦ Medals
Roman and Ancient Coins
Coins of the World ♦ Fossils
Ancient Pottery ♦ Militaria
Cigarette Cards ♦ Postcards
Metal Detectors ♦ Accessories
Banknotes

MONDAY-SATURDAY 10am-5pm

VISIT OUR WEB SITE
http://members.aol.com/coingranta/index.html

ALL MAJOR CREDIT CARDS ACCEPTED

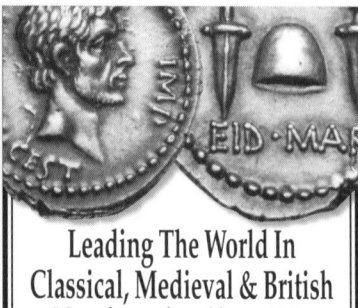

Classical Numismatic Group, Inc.

Leading The World In Classical, Medieval & British Numismatics, Since 1975

Auctions, Fixed Price Lists & Private Treaty Sales,
Complimentary Catalogue On Request

CNG
Classical Numismatic Group, Inc.

14 Old Bond Street, London W1X 3DB U. K.
Tel: **(0207) 495-1888** Fax: **(0207) 499-5916**
E-Mail: cng@historicalcoins.com
Web Site: www.historicalcoins.com

Treasure Hunting
BRITAIN'S BEST SELLING METAL DETECTING MAGAZINE

A fascinating read about this great hobby. You don't have to own a detector to find a wealth of information and pleasure in the pages of Treasure Hunting.

AVAILABLE FROM GOOD NEWSAGENTS

Call **01376 521900** *for a sample copy or the latest subscription offers*

Greenlight Publishing, 119 Newland Street, Witham, Essex CM8 1WF
Tel: 01376 521900 Fax: 01376 521901
www.treasurehunting.co.uk

EDINBURGH COIN SHOP
Scotland's leading dealer

Large stocks of British and World coins

6-8 COIN AUCTIONS EACH YEAR

Also auctions of medals, banknotes, stamps and cigarette cards

Write, phone or fax for your FREE catalogue

FREE VALUATIONS

11 West Crosscauseway,
Edinburgh EH8 9JW
Tel: **0131 668 2928** *or* **0131 667 9095**
Fax: **0131 668 2926**

Giessener Münzhandlung

A partner that sets itself above the rest

✗ because we are always paying fair prices

✗ because competent advice is one of our strengths

✗ because our large inventory offers you the widest of selections

✗ because we hold four auctions yearly including Ancient, Medieval and Modern coins

✗ because we will accept your consignment of coins and / or medals at any time

✗ because you can take our guarantee of authenticity for granted

- Buying
- Selling
- Counselling
- Evaluations
- Auctions

Giessener Münzhandlung
Dieter Gorny GmbH

Maximiliansplatz 20
D-80333 München
Tel: 089 - 24 22 643-0
Fax: 089 - 22 85 513

Office hours:
Monday – Friday
10:00am - 1:00pm
2:30pm - 6:00pm

GERMAN AND WORLD BANKNOTES

BUYING AND SELLING

We issue irregular lists of German and World Banknotes (just call or write for a current list).

We attend major shows all over the world, trying to purchase all types of notes (and coins) to supply our clients.

We need to buy your one note or your complete collection or accumulation.

We will be happy to appraise or make an obligation-free offer for your material. (We believe that when you want to sell, our offer will be accepted.)

We even purchase outdated currency notes from almost every country.

We always need German notgeld, all US notes, as well as the things everyone else wants.

We simply want to either supply you with nice, fairly priced Banknotes; or purchase the same from you.

For fair, prompt, professional service – try us; you'll be glad you did!

PHILIP PHIPPS
P.O. Box 31, Emsworth, Hants
PO10 8XA, UK

Tel/Fax: +44 - 01243 376086
Mobile: +44 - 0850 864554

The Royal Mint: A Tradition of Excellence

An invitation to join the Royal Mint Coin Club

Coin collecting is now one of the most keenly pursued hobbies in the world. In order to satisfy the demands of the modern collector, the Royal Mint has established its own Coin Club to provide its members with the latest information on new coins from both home and abroad. Recognised as the supreme examples of the minter's art, Royal Mint collector coins, often struck in precious metals, form a tangible record of our heritage.

To find out more about how coins are created and to receive your free brochures, simply telephone [01443] **623456** or write to the address below for further information.

Royal Mint Coin Club
FREEPOST,
PO Box 500 Cardiff CF1 1YY

ROYAL MINT

BRITISH BANK NOTES
Bank of England, Treasury, White Notes

Scotland
Ireland
Channel Islands
Isle of Man

Plus much more

We also organise paper money fairs *at*
The Bonnington Hotel, London WC1
FEBRUARY, MAY, SEPTEMBER, NOVEMBER

BUYING WHITE FIVERS

British Bank Note List free on request
Buying all aspects of British notes

PAM WEST,
PO Box 257
Sutton, Surrey, England SM3 9WW
Tel/Fax: 0181 641 3224

ANCIENT COIN SPECIALIST

Celtic, Roman, Saxon,
Medieval Coins &
Associated Small Antiques

ALL AT PRICES LESS HURTFUL THAN MOST

Please send for fully illustrated catalogue

PHIL GOODWIN

PO Box 69, Portsmouth,
Hants PO1 5SH
TEL: 01705-423267
or 01705-752006 (incl. fax)

MAHOGANY COIN CABINETS

Pheon Classic
From £129

Mascle Classic
From £79

I manufacture a range of 15 coin and medal cabinets priced from just £30 to £350

All cabinets are crafted and polished from selected mahogany, mounted and fitted with brass furniture. Trays are available with a full range of coin sizes from crowns to farthings.

As supplier to the world's leading international museums the timber I use conforms to their exact specifications and is sourced from suppliers with an active re-planting policy.

With over 30 years' experience I am sure that I can supply a cabinet to suit your requirements.

For a full descriptive leaflet of my range please contact:

PETER NICHOLS
Cabinet Maker
3 Norman Road, St Leonard's on Sea
East Sussex TN37 6NH
Tel: 01424 436682

COINCRAFT
Your one-stop-shop for numismatics!

• British & world coins • British & world banknotes
• tokens • antiquities

If your interest is numismatics, then **we** are here to help you

• Call in and see our two shops • Or write for a *free* copy of our regular numismatics collectibles newspaper, *The Phoenix*

Open Monday to Friday 9.30am-5pm
Saturday 10.00am-2.30pm

COINCRAFT
Opposite the British Museum
44 & 45 Great Russell Street, London WC1B 3LU
Tel: 0207 636 1188 • 0207 637 8785
Fax: 0207 323 2860 • 0207 637 7635
Email: info@coincraft.com

London Coin Auctions

ARE YOU SELLING?

- Do you want your material professionally graded, advertised and marketed?
- Do you want to offer your material to over 400 dealers and collectors here and abroad without leaving your home?
- Do you want to receive 90% of what your material sells for?

THEN YOU SHOULD SEND FOR A COPY OF OUR VENDOR DETAILS.

ARE YOU BUYING?

- Do you want to receive accurately graded coins?
  - Do you want to dictate the price you pay, rather than a dealer's retail list?
- Do you want to peruse a list of several thousand items for sale from dealers and collectors from all over the world without going anywhere?

THEN YOU SHOULD BE ON OUR MAILING LIST.

LCA, 31 Reigate Way, Wallington, Surrey SM6 8NU
Phone 0181 688 5297   Fax 0181 680 8071

Successfully bringing together buyers and sellers of all coins and banknotes – any era, any country.

---

numistory.com

QUALITY HAMMERED
AND EARLY MILLED ENGLISH COINS

Online Catalogs

with high resolution colour images

ALSO A FINE SELECTION OF ANCIENT, MEDIEVAL AND RENAISSANCE COINS

Andy Singer	Phil Wallick III
PO Box 235	PO Box 61
Greenbelt, MD	Simpsonville, MD
USA 20768	USA 21150
Tel: 301-805-7085	Tel: 410-381-5124
Email: andy@numistory.com	Email: philw3@numistory.com

FORMAT COINS
FOR BRITISH AND FOREIGN COINS

The only British Members of the I.A.P.N based in Birmingham. For over a quarter of a century we have been dealing in coins of the world. We need to buy English and Foreign coins to offer to our regular sales lists.

If you have coins for sale, or would like to receive our sales lists, please contact:

GARRY CHARMAN OR DAVID VICE
FORMAT of BIRMINGHAM LTD
18/19 BENNETTS HILL,
BIRMINGHAM, B2 5QJ
ENGLAND
Tel: 0121-643 2058
Fax: 0121-643 2210

Opening Hours 9.30am–5.00pm Monday–Friday

MEMBERS OF I.A.P.N. & B.N.T.A.

NORWAY

COINS AND BANK NOTES

If you are interested in coins and/or banknotes from Norway, please contact us.
We would appreciate being your contact in Norway.

Ask for our World banknote lists.

We are publishing the yearly Catalogue
"Norwegian Banknotes"
1877 – 2000
Now with all notes in colour.

Mynt & Seddel

P.O. Box 779 – Sentrum, N-5807 Bergen, Norway
Tlf.: + 47 55 31 96 31, Fax.: + 47 55 31 95 70
E-mail: myntseda@online.no
www.myntogseddel.hl.no

Discover the Beauty Within...

For expert, impartial advice on the history, condition, rarity and market appeal of coins, why not contact the oldest established coin business in the world?

At Spink, you can buy and sell coins from ancient to modern; medals, tokens, banknotes and bullion; orders, decorations and campaign medals, stamps and books.

Please contact us for details of our regular auctions, and for your complimentary copy of *The Numismatic Circular, Banknote Circular and Medal Circular*, our magazines offering items for sale at fixed prices. Please ask for details of *The Philatelist*, our journal featuring articles, reviews and previews.

For impartial advice and unrivalled expertise, please telephone or visit. We are open Monday-Friday from 9.00am to 5.30pm. Our coin department can be contacted on Tel: 0171 747 6834/020 7747 6834 Fax: 0171 839 4853/ 020 7839 4853. E-mail: spink@btinternet.com (Please quote ref. CC1)

'The Three Graces' –
*George III Pattern Crown in Gold, 1817,
From The Herman Selig Collection Part II,
Sold for a record price of £170,500
on 2nd March 1999.*

SPINK
founded 1666

5 KING STREET, ST JAMES'S, LONDON SW1Y 6QS.

MICHAEL COINS

We have a retail shop – established for over 30 years. Can we help you?

We stock all grades of coins and from the common to the extremely rare.

We stock British as well as coins from most world countries. Even some Ancients and Hammered. We specialise in British Copper and Bronze varieties.

We publish the reference book on 'The British Bronze Penny 1860-1970'.

We also have a large stock of British and world banknotes and accessories.

Open Tues-Fri 10.00am-5.00pm
(Outside these hours by appointment)

6 Hillgate Street
Notting Hill Gate, London W8 7SR
Tel/Fax: 0207 727 1518

BANK OF ENGLAND MUSEUM

Threadneedle Street
(entrance in Bartholomew Lane)
London EC2R 8AH
Tel: 0207 601 5545
Fax: 0207 601 5808

Open Monday - Friday throughout the year
10.00 - 17.00

Closed Weekends and Public Bank Holidays

ADMISSION FREE

A fascinating insight into the world of banking & money from the Bank of England's foundation in 1694 to the present day.

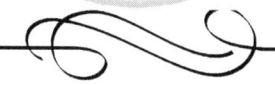

WANTED: ALL UNITED STATES GOLD COINS

We are one of the largest buyers and importers of U.S. Gold Coins from Europe and the rest of the world. We are also interested in purchasing Coins & Banknotes from Japan, Korea, Thailand and Hong Kong. We offer TOP competitive prices on all U.S. Gold coins, especially $5, $10 and $20 gold pieces.

AUCTIONS

Taisei – Baldwin – Gillio
Singapore   Hong Kong   U.K.   U.S.A.

Butterfield – Johnson – Gillio
San Francisco   Los Angeles

COINS – BANKNOTES – MEDALLIONS

Top prices paid for outright purchase or auction in the U.S. and Far East
We hold auctions in the U.S. at the galleries of Butterfield: Butterfield in Los Angeles or San Francisco; and in Hong Kong and Singapore in conjunction with Taisei-Baldwin-Gillio
We have been conducting auctions in the Far East since 1982; and in the U.S. since 1967
We have representatives in Europe who can view any material, usually within 24 hours
Please contact our office in Santa Barbara for further information

RONALD J. GILLIO, INC
GILLIO COINS ASIA LTD, HONG KONG
1103 STATE STREET, SANTA BARBARA, CALIF. 93101 USA
Phone (805) 963-1345; Fax (805) 962-6659

American Numismatic Association Life Member No.950 since 1964

COINOTE SERVICES LTD

SPECIALISING IN COINS & BANKNOTES FROM MID 1600 TO DATE.

BOOKS AND ACCESSORIES. LARGE SELECTION OF CHEAPER COINS.

FREE WORLD COIN AND BANKNOTE LISTS AVAILABLE.

Phone 01429 273044 / Fax 01429 272411
Mobile 0589 119363

MOST CREDIT CARDS TAKEN.

FULL WEB SITE WITH SECURE SERVER AND PGP ENCRYPTION

Web site: mastmedia.co.uk/coinote

E-mail: paul@coinote-services.freeserve.co.uk

Postal address:
PO Box 53, Sorting Office, Clarke Street,
Hartlepool, England TS26 9YL

The World's Largest Rare Coin Dealer

Buying
Selling
Auctioning...

Our Numismatists stand ready to help <u>you</u> sell your rare coins, currency or bullion.

We want to spend almost $3,000,000 every week.
We also offer complete Want List Services. Call us about our E-Listing program.

HERITAGE RARE COIN GALLERIES

HERITAGE Numismatic Auctions, Inc. America's Convention Auctioneer

Contact Our Consignor Hotline at
1-800 US COINS (872-6467) ext. 222
e-mail: bids@heritagecoin.com • FAX: 214-4438425
Visit our Website: www.heritagecoin.com

Regular Coin Sales

Five Guineas — Charles II (1660 – 1685)

No.	Date	Features	Edge date	Obv. Rev.	F	
C25GM-005	1668		VICESIMO	1 1	900	1
C25GM-010	1668	elephant below head	VICESIMO	1 1	900	1
C25GM-015			VICESIMO PRIMO	1 1	950	1
C25GM-			VICESIMO PRIMO	1 1	1100	2
C2			VICESIMO SECVNDO	1 1	950	1
C2			VICESIMO TERTIO	1 1	950	1
C2			VICESIMO QVARTO	1 1	950	1
C25G			VICESIMO QVINTO	1 1	950	1
C25GM-045			VICESIMO	1 1	950	1
C25GM-050	1675	2		1	950	1
C25GM-055	1675	el b		1	950	1
C25GM-060	1675	a c h		1	1200	2
C25GM-065	1676	3		1	950	1
C25GM-070	1676			1	950	1
C25GM-075	1676	elephant and		1 1	950	1

A 1668 "Elephant" coinage Five-Guinea piece of Charles II, from a small private collection sold at Bonhams in March, 1999 for £4,255.

The art of preparating an auction catalogue is a skill that requires more than just expertise, knowledge and integrity. At Bonhams our coin catalogues present the facts in a precise, accurate and easy to follow style. Many pieces are illustrated, and *Standard Catalogue* references are given for individual coins.

Our quarterly sales contain a fascinating mixture of ancient to modern coins, from Greek and Roman issues to coins of the modern world, also Historical medals, War medals and Decorations.

For a Free Auction Valuation, or further information about buying or selling a single item or a whole collection, please call Daniel Fearon or Paul Hill of the Coin & Medal Department.

0171 393 3949

or e-mail: coins@bonhams.com

BONHAMS
AUCTIONEERS & VALUERS SINCE 1793

Montpelier Street, London SW7 1HH. Tel: 0171 393 3900 Fax: 0171 393 3905
Internet: www.bonhams.com

- ANCIENT COINS • MEDIEVAL COINS •
- • MODERN COINS •
- • ODD & CURIOUS MONIES •
- • TOKENS AND MEDALS • WORLD PAPER MONEY •
- • COINS OF THE BIBLE • PALESTINE AND ISRAEL •

Specialists in the Numismatics of the Jewish people and the Holy Land from Ancient to Modern Times

- PRICE LISTS • MAIL BIDS • SHOWS •
- • MUSEUM CONSULTATIONS • APPRAISALS •

Instructor at the ANA Summer Conference

Serving the collector since 1971

BUY – SELL – TRADE

WILLIAM M. ROSENBLUM RARE COINS
P.O. BOX 355
EVERGREEN, CO 80437-0355 USA
PHONE 303-838-4831 FAX 303-838-1213
E-MAIL: wmrcoins@qadas.com

PATRICK FINN
Numismatist

Specialist in Early British Scottish, Irish and Anglo-Gallic Coins

I offer good quality, fully illustrated, lists of coins for sale three times a year. I have nearly 40 years of experience in the marketplace and am able to provide the best advice on English hammered coins, and all Scottish and Irish coins.

Write for a complimentary copy of my lists and find out what you have been missing.

PATRICK FINN *Numismatist*
P.O. Box 26
Kendal, Cumbria LA9 7AB.
Telephone: 01539 730008
Fax: 01539 721800

COINS ON THE INTERNET

www.netcollect.co.uk

e-mail

enquiries@netcollect.co.uk

post

Littlemill Media,
Hobsley House, Frodesley,
Shrewsbury SY5 7HD, UK

telephone

01743 272140
01686 640599

Chelsea Coins
DIMITRI LOULAKAKIS
PROFESSIONAL NUMISMATIST SINCE 1966

Specialising in all European coins, medieval to modern day. Modern Greek, French, Italian, Russian, German and, of course, British. Specialist in Maundy Sets and all numismatic gold.

We can communicate in English, Greek, Italian and French.

We attend all the London auctions and can execute bids on your behalf. Callers by appointment only. Telephone between 10:00 and 20:00.

Chelsea Coins
P.O. BOX 2, FULHAM ROAD
LONDON SW10 9PQ

TEL: 0044181-870-5501
FAX: 0044181-875-1459

Mark Davidson

(Postal Address Only)

P.O.Box 197
South Croydon
Surrey CR2 0ZD
Telephone: 0181-651 3890

❧ ☙

Buying and Selling Coins
especially English Hammered

Please request a catalogue of hammered coins for sale.

Valuations for insurance and probate undertaken.

RODERICK RICHARDSON
(Specialist in English Hammered & Early Milled)

Expert advice
Provenance searches
Photography
Valuations

Wanted
Charles I Provincial mint collections

Individual items

These and many others for sale
For details or to join my mailing list:
The Old Granary Antiques Centre, King's Staithe Lane, King's Lynn, Norfolk PE30 1LZ
Tel & Fax: (01553) 670833 Tel: (01553) 775509
Internet address: http://coin.dealers-on-line.com/roderick

Coins at Auction

We are currently accepting Ancient Greek, Roman, hammered and milled coins of the world for inclusion in our forthcoming sales.

If you have an item or collection and would like a valuation, with view to selling at auction, please call Andrew Litherland on (0171) 493 2445.

All advice is given in complete confidence and without obligation.

101 New Bond Street,
London W1Y 9LG.
Tel : (0171) 493 2445

Glendining's

http: www.phillips-auctions.com

A North American specialist firm

We buy better British coins and tokens

We regularly issue serious catalogs

Major mail auction sales of choice classic British and Ancient material
(no buyer's fee)

Write, call or fax for a sample of our current catalog

Over 20 years as North America's leading professionals for British coins and tokens

Davissons Ltd.

Cold Spring, MN 56320 • USA
320-685-3835,
24 hour FAX 320-685-8636
email: DAVCOIN@AOL.COM

THE LONDON COIN FAIR

LARGEST UK NUMISMATIC SHOW
80 SPECIALIST DEALERS IN ANCIENT & MODERN COINS, PAPER MONEY, MEDALS, TOKENS, BOOKS AND ANTIQUITIES

THE CUMBERLAND HOTEL
Marble Arch, London W1, England

11 September 1999	6 November 1999
5 February 2000	3 June 2000
9 September 2000	4 November 2000

Admission £3 (Concessions £1.50) 9.30am-5pm

Information: **SIMMONS GALLERY**
53 LAMBS CONDUIT ST, LONDON WC1N 3NB
Tel: 0171-831 2080   Fax: 0171-831 2090

HSBC Money Gallery

The world's finest display of money from the earliest evidence of exchange to the present day

The 'Juxon Medal'
five pound pattern of Charles I,
one of the many unique pieces in the gallery

Admission Free
Open 10.00-17.00 Monday-Saturday
12.00-18.00 Sunday

For enquiries about the HSBC Money Gallery and the Department of Coins and Medals' Students Room and services
Telephone 0171 323 8404

BRITISH MUSEUM
GREAT RUSSELL STREET • LONDON WC1B 3DG

Looking for your nearest coin club?

The British Association of Numismatic Societies

can help you

With over 60 affiliated societies throughout the UK, we can usually put you in touch with a club near you

For this and other information on BANS, please contact the Secretary:

British Association of
Numismatic Societies
c/o Bush Boake Allen Ltd
Blackhorse Lane
London E17 5QP
Phone: 0181 523 6531
email: phil_mernick@bushboakeallen.com

COIN FAIR
KNAVESMIRE STAND
(MEZZANINE LEVEL)
YORK RACECOURSE

Featuring:
- ★ Coins
- ★ Medals
- ★ Accessories
- ★ Banknotes
- ★ Tokens
- ★ Publications, etc

2000 DATES
FRIDAY JANUARY 14th 11am - 6pm
SATURDAY JANUARY 15th 10am - 5pm

FRIDAY JULY 28th 11am - 6pm
SATURDAY JULY 29th 10am - 5pm

40 Dealers

AA signposted

For information ring 01268 726687
0181 946 4489 or 01425 656459
www.stampshows.co.uk

ANTHONY HALSE

Wide selection of coins for sale from budget-priced date fillers to coins for the advanced collector.

Postal only

Send for free list:

The Headlands,
Chepstow Road,
Langstone, Newport,
Gwent NP6 2JN

Tel: 01633 413238
Mobile: 0378 999838

SOUTH AFRICA

We offer a wide variety of services and can cater for all of your coin requirements.

No order too large or small. We aim to please and strive for perfection and excellence in service – please contact **Gary Levitan today!**

ROYAL GOLD EXCHANGE
PO Box 123
Saxonwold
Johannesburg 2132
South Africa
Tel: +27 11 442 4321
Fax: +27 11 442 4035
E-mail address:
royalg@iafrica.com

- Buying
- Selling
- Gold
- Modern

COIN FAIR
at
Commonwealth Institute
Kensington High Street, London W8
(Entrance through car park)

1999
October 23rd   November 27th
18th December

2000
January 22nd   February 17th
March 18th   April 8th
May 13th   June 17th

9.30am–3.00pm
Admission £1

★ ★ ★ ★ ★ ★

Dealers in English, Foreign, Ancient, Antiquities,
Tokens, Medallions and Banknotes

Enquiries: Davidson Monk Fairs
Tel: 0181-656 4583 or 0181 651 3890

Dates correct at time of publication.
Please check with organisers.

SAFE Coin System NOVA
A star in both price and quality.

- light, portable and compact
- round and rectangular range
- space saving
- elegant design
- suitable for secure storage
- stackable

Dimensions:
250 x 195 mm
(9¼ x 7¾)

POST + PACKING COSTS
One tray add   £ 2.50
Two trays add   £ 4.25
Three trays add £ 5.00
Four trays add £ 6.00
Five trays add £ 7.00
6 TRAYS + POST FREE!

Price per inset £ 9.75 each + postage (see panel)

The SAFE-Coin System NOVA™ is obtainable with the following Special Trays:

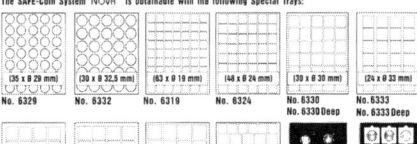

(35 x Ø 29 mm)	(30 x Ø 32,5 mm)	(63 x Ø 19 mm)	(46 x Ø 24 mm)	(30 x Ø 30 mm)	(24 x Ø 33 mm)
No. 6329	No. 6332	No. 6319	No. 6324	No. 6330 / No. 6330 Deep	No. 6333 / No. 6333 Deep
(20 x Ø 38 mm)	(20 x Ø 38 mm)	(20 x Ø 41 mm)	(Ø 23, 28, 31, 34, 36, 39 mm)	(70 x Ø 62 mm)	(12 x Ø 50 mm)
No. 6336 / No. 6336 Deep	No. 6338 / No. 6338 Deep	No. 6341 / No. 6341 Deep	No. 6368 / No. 6368 Deep	No. 6370	No. 6350

Note - Ref. Nos with word Deep, means trays are suitable for coins already in Acrylic case.

SAFE Albums (UK)LTD • 16 Falcon Business Park • 38 Ivanhoe Road •
Finchampstead • Berkshire • RG40 4QQ • Tel. (0118) 932 8976 • Fax (0118) 932 8612

Dorset Coin Co Ltd.
BNTA Member   IBNS Member   FSB Member
193 ASHLEY ROAD, PARKSTONE,
POOLE, DORSET BH14 9DL
Tel: 01202 739606 Fax: 01202 739230

WE ISSUE REGULAR
COIN & BANKNOTE LISTS
INCLUDING...

- British Coins and Banknotes
- British and Foreign Gold Coins
- Gold Coin Sets
- Proofs and Proof sets
- Foreign Coins and Banknotes
- Tokens
- Medals
- Medallions

**WE BUY COLLECTIONS/
ACCUMULATIONS
OF ALL COINS AND BANKNOTES
INCLUDING ALL GOLD, SILVER AND
COPPER COINS**

Callers Welcome Mon–Fri 9am–4pm

ANCIENT COINS & ANTIQUITIES

Bronze-age, Celtic, Roman, Saxon, Viking,
Medieval, Greek, Egyptian + many others

For illustrated sales
catalogue please
tel/fax or write to:

The Den of
Antiquity

tel/fax: 01353 741 759

26 West End, Haddenham,
Cambs CB6 3TE, UK

If You Love World Coins
WORLD COIN UNIVERSE™
Is Your Ultimate Internet Destination

Go to World Coin Universe for:

Auctions – Daily and Weekly
Collectors Auctions...Hold your own auction or buy from other collectors.

World Coin Universe Certified Auctions... Weekly auctions of rare PCGS, NGC and ANACS certifed world coins.

The Ultimate World Coin Collectors Internet Destination!

COLLECTORS UNIVERSE™•COM
The Ultimate Collectors Destination™

MAKE MONEY • HAVE FUN • LOG ON TODAY!

Go to: www.Collectors.com Click on WORLD COINS

Would you like to see your book on the shelf?

Have you ever thought of writing a book on some area of numismatics? Have you written a book but not yet had it published? Have you always wanted to see your work in print? Well here may be your chance to make your wish a reality...

Standard Catalogue Publishers Ltd, a division of Coincraft, are interested in publishing books on coins, medals, tokens or paper money. Having already gained world-wide recognition as the publishers of Coincraft Standard Catalogues, we are now looking to publish other similar works that have a broad numismatic appeal.

If you would like to see your work published, please submit a brief outline or synopsis of your proposal to: *Dr Eleni Calligas, editor at Standard Catalogue Publishers Ltd.*

Standard Catalogue Publishers Ltd

c/o Coincraft
44 & 45 Great Russell Street
London WC1B 3LU

Tel: (0207) 636 1188 : (0207) 637 8785
Fax: (0207) 637 7635 : (0207) 323 2860

Email: info@coincraft.com

Five Guineas

Charles II (1660 – 1685)

✓	No.	Date	Features	Grade	Purchased From	Date	Price Paid	Value Now
	C25GM-005	1668						
	C25GM-010	1668	elephant below head					
	C25GM-015	1669						
	C25GM-020	1669	elephant below head					
	C25GM-025	1670						
	C25GM-030	1671						
	C25GM-035	1672						
	C25GM-040	1673						
	C25GM-045	1674						
	C25GM-050	1675						
	C25GM-055	1675	elephant below head					
	C25GM-060	1675	elephant and castle below head					
	C25GM-065	1676	edge VICESIMO SEPTIMO					
	C25GM-070	1676	edge VICESIMO OCTAVO					
	C25GM-075	1676	elephant and castle below head					
	C25GM-080	1677						
	C25GM-085	1677	elephant and castle below head; edge VICESIMO OCTAVO					
	C25GM-090	1678						
	C25GM-095	1678	8 over 7					
	C25GM-100	1678	elephant and castle below head; 8 over 7					
	C25GM-105	1678	8 over 7					
	C25GM-110	1679						
	C25GM-115	1680						
	C25GM-120	1680	elephant and castle below head					
	C25GM-125	1681						
	C25GM-130	1681	elephant and castle below head					
	C25GM-135	1682						
	C25GM-140	1682	elephant and castle below head					
	C25GM-145	1683						
	C25GM-150	1683	elephant and castle below head					
	C25GM-155	1684						
	C25GM-160	1684	elephant and castle below head					

James II (1685 – 1688)

✓	No.	Date	Features	Grade	Purchased From	Date	Price Paid	Value Now
	J25G-005	1686						
	J25G-010	1687	obv. 1					
	J25G-015	1687	elephant and castle below head; obv. 1					
	J25G-020	1687	obv. 2					
	J25G-025	1688	obv. 1					

Cont.

Coincraft's Coin Checklist

✓	No.	Date	Features	Grade	Purchased From	Date	Price Paid	Value Now
	J25G-030	1688	elephant and castle below head; obv. 1					
	J25G-035	1688	obv. 2					

William & Mary (1688 – 1694)

✓	No.	Date	Features	Grade	Purchased From	Date	Price Paid	Value Now
	WM5G-005	1691						
	WM5G-010	1691	elephant and castle below head					
	WM5G-015	1692						
	WM5G-020	1692	elephant and castle below head					
	WM5G-025	1693						
	WM5G-030	1693	elephant and castle below head					
	WM5G-035	1694						
	WM5G-040	1694	4 over indeterminate figure					
	WM5G-045	1694	elephant and castle below head					
	WM5G-050	1694	elephant and castle below head; 4 over indeterminate figure					

William III (1695 – 1701)

✓	No.	Date	Features	Grade	Purchased From	Date	Price Paid	Value Now
	W35G-005	1699						
	W35G-010	1699	elephant and castle below head					
	W35G-015	1700						
	W35G-020	1701						
	W35G-025	1701						

Anne (1702 – 1714)

✓	No.	Date	Features	Grade	Purchased From	Date	Price Paid	Value Now
	A5G-005	1703	VIGO below head; stops on obverse					
	A5G-010	1703	VIGO below head; no stops on obverse					
	A5G-015	1705						
	A5G-020	1706	rev. 1					
	A5G-025	1706	rev. 2					
	A5G-030	1709						
	A5G-035	1711						
	A5G-040	1713						
	A5G-045	1714						
	A5G-050	1714	4 over 1 or 3					

George I (1714 – 1727)

✓	No.	Date	Features	Grade	Purchased From	Date	Price Paid	Value Now
	G15G-005	1716						
	G15G-010	1717						

Cont.

Five Guineas

√	No.	Date	Features	Grade	Purchased From	Date	Price Paid	Value Now
	G15G-015	1717	D of DECVS inverted (edge)					
	G15G-020	1720						
	G15G-025	1726						
	G15G-030	1726	each N on edge inverted (top left of N has no serif)					

George II (1727 – 1760)

√	No.	Date	Features	Grade	Purchased From	Date	Price Paid	Value Now
	G25G-005	1729						
	G25G-010	1729	PROOF; edge plain					
	G25G-015	1729	EIC below head					
	G25G-020	1731						
	G25G-025	1731	PROOF					
	G25G-030	1735						
	G25G-035	1738						
	G25G-040	1741						
	G25G-045	1741	41 over 35					
	G25G-050	1746	LIMA below head					
	G25G-055	1748						
	G25G-060	1753						

Fifty Shillings

Oliver Cromwell
(Commonwealth 1649 – 1660)

✓	No.	Date	Features	Grade	Purchased From	Date	Price Paid	Value Now
	CR50S-005	1656						

Two Guineas

Charles II (1660 – 1685)

✓	No.	Date	Features	Grade	Purchased From	Date	Price Paid	Value Now
	C22GM-005	1664						
	C22GM-010	1664	elephant below head					
	C22GM-015	1665						
	C22GM-020	1669						
	C22GM-025	1671						
	C22GM-030	1675						
	C22GM-035	1676						
	C22GM-040	1676	elephant and castle below head					
	C22GM-045	1677						
	C22GM-050	1678	usually or always 8 over 7					
	C22GM-055	1678	elephant below head					
	C22GM-060	1678	elephant and castle below head					
	C22GM-065	1679						
	C22GM-070	1680						
	C22GM-075	1681						
	C22GM-080	1682						
	C22GM-085	1682	elephant and castle below head					
	C22GM-090	1683						
	C22GM-095	1683	elephant and castle below head					
	C22GM-100	1684						
	C22GM-105	1684	elephant and castle below head					

James II (1685 – 1688)

✓	No.	Date	Features	Grade	Purchased From	Date	Price Paid	Value Now
	J22G-005	1687						
	J22G-010	1688	usually or always 8 over 7					

William & Mary (1688 – 1694)

✓	No.	Date	Features	Grade	Purchased From	Date	Price Paid	Value Now
	WM2G-005	1691	elephant and castle below head					
	WM2G-010	1693						
	WM2G-015	1693	elephant and castle below head					
	WM2G-020	1694	usually or always 4 over 3					
	WM2G-025	1694	elephant and castle below head; usually or always 4 over 3					

William III (1695 – 1701)

✓	No.	Date	Features	Grade	Purchased From	Date	Price Paid	Value Now
	W32G-005	1701						

Coincraft's Coin Checklist

Anne (1702 – 1714)

✓	No.	Date	Features	Grade	Purchased From	Date	Price Paid	Value Now
	A2G-005	1709						
	A2G-010	1711						
	A2G-015	1713						
	A2G-020	1714						
	A2G-025	1714	4 over 1 or 3					

George I (1714 – 1727)

✓	No.	Date	Features	Grade	Purchased From	Date	Price Paid	Value Now
	G12G-005	1717						
	G12G-010	1720						
	G12G-012	1720	0 over 1					
	G12G-015	1726						

George II (1727 – 1760)

✓	No.	Date	Features	Grade	Purchased From	Date	Price Paid	Value Now
	G22G-005	1734	4 over 3					
	G22G-010	1735						
	G22G-015	1738						
	G22G-020	1739	obv. 1					
	G22G-025	1739	obv. 2					
	G22G-030	1740						
	G22G-032	1740	4 over 3 or 40 over 39					
	G22G-035	1748						
	G22G-040	1753						

Get your *free* copy of The Phoenix

The Phoenix, the only monthly coin, banknote and antiquities newspaper in the UK!

- 24 tabloid-sized pages
- Hundreds of items on offer
- British and World Coins
- British and World Banknotes
- Greek & Roman Coins
- Greek, Roman and Egyptian antiquities
- Special offers and discounts
- Hundreds of photographs in every issue

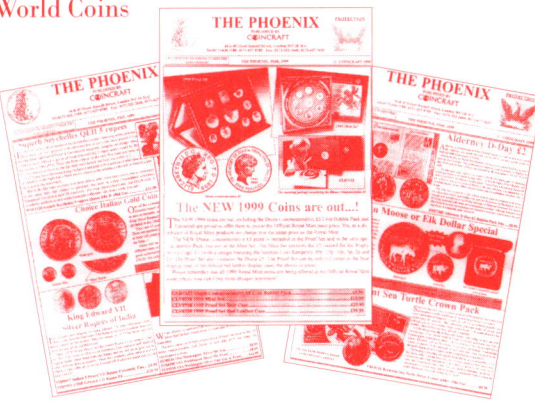

Coincraft is a family firm which has dealt in coins for over 40 years. At Coincraft we believe in old fashioned values; such as the collector is always right, even when occasionally he or she is wrong!

ORDER WITH CONFIDENCE!

Our guarantee to you

All items listed in *The Phoenix* are guaranteed authentic. If for any reason you are dissatisfied with anything ordered from *The Phoenix*, simply return it to us in undamaged condition within 30 days for a full no-questions-asked refund.

We have total confidence in the goods we sell.
We want YOU to have total confidence in us!

Please send me a complimentary copy of *The Phoenix* – your monthly catalogue of British and World Coins, British and World Banknotes, ancient coins, medals, tokens and antiquities.

NAME ....

ADDRESS ....

....

....

....

POSTCODE .... COUNTRY ....

CCC0900

Get your *free* copy of The Phoenix

The Phoenix, the only monthly coin, banknote and antiquities newspaper in the UK!

- 24 tabloid-sized pages
- Hundreds of items on offer
- British and World Coins
- British and World Banknotes
- Greek and Roman Coins
- Greek, Roman and Egyptian antiquities
- Special offers and discounts
- Hundreds of photographs in every issue

Coincraft is a family firm which has dealt in coins for over 40 years. At Coincraft we believe in old fashioned values; such as the collector is always right, even when occasionally he or she is wrong!

By Air Mail
Par Avion

Please place stamp here

The Phoenix
c/o Coincraft
44 & 45 Great Russell Street
London WC1B 3LU
UK

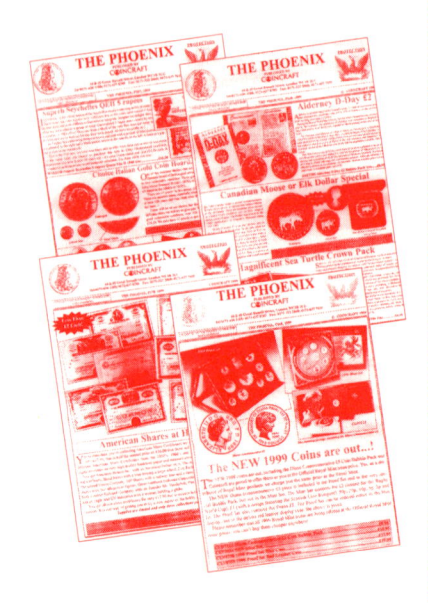

Broad

Oliver Cromwell (Commonwealth 1649 – 1660)

✓	No.	Date	Features	Grade	Purchased From	Date	Price Paid	Value Now
	CRBR-005	1656						

Guinea

Charles II (1660 – 1685)

✓	No.	Date	Features	Grade	Purchased From	Date	Price Paid	Value Now
	C2GNM-005	1663						
	C2GNM-010	1663	elephant below head					
	C2GNM-015	1664	obv. 2					
	C2GNM-020	1664	elephant below head; obv. 2					
	C2GNM-025	1664	obv. 3					
	C2GNM-030	1664	elephant below head; obv. 3					
	C2GNM-035	1665						
	C2GNM-040	1665	elephant below head					
	C2GNM-045	1666						
	C2GNM-050	1667						
	C2GNM-055	1668						
	C2GNM-060	1668	elephant below head					
	C2GNM-065	1669						
	C2GNM-070	1670						
	C2GNM-075	1671						
	C2GNM-080	1672	obv. 3					
	C2GNM-085	1672	obv. 4					
	C2GNM-090	1673	obv. 3					
	C2GNM-095	1673	obv. 4					
	C2GNM-100	1673	CRAOLVS instead of CAROLVS (obv.); obv. 4					
	C2GNM-105	1674						
	C2GNM-110	1674	elephant and castle below head					
	C2GNM-115	1675						
	C2GNM-120	1675	CRAOLVS instead of CAROLVS (obv.)					
	C2GNM-125	1675	elephant and castle below head					
	C2GNM-130	1676						
	C2GNM-135	1676	elephant and castle below head					
	C2GNM-140	1677						
	C2GNM-145	1677	elephant below head latter 7 over 5					
	C2GNM-150	1677	elephant and castle below head					
	C2GNM-155	1678						
	C2GNM-160	1678	elephant below head					
	C2GNM-165	1678	elephant and castle below head					
	C2GNM-170	1679						
	C2GNM-175	1679	elephant and castle below head					
	C2GNM-180	1680						
	C2GNM-185	1680	elephant and castle below head					
	C2GNM-190	1681						
	C2GNM-195	1681	elephant and castle below head					
	C2GNM-200	1682						
	C2GNM-205	1682	rev. →					
	C2GNM-210	1682	elephant and castle below head					
	C2GNM-215	1683						
	C2GNM-220	1683	elephant and castle below head					

Cont.

Guinea

✓	No.	Date	Features	Grade	Purchased From	Date	Price Paid	Value Now
	C2GNM-225	1684						
	C2GNM-230	1684	elephant and castle below head					

James II (1685 – 1688)

✓	No.	Date	Features	Grade	Purchased From	Date	Price Paid	Value Now
	J2GN-005	1685						
	J2GN-010	1685	elephant and castle below head					
	J2GN-015	1686	obv. 1					
	J2GN-020	1686	elephant and castle below head; obv. 1					
	J2GN-025	1686	obv. 2					
	J2GN-030	1686	elephant and castle below head; obv. 2					
	J2GN-035	1687						
	J2GN-040	1687	7 over 6					
	J2GN-045	1687	elephant and castle below head					
	J2GN-050	1688						
	J2GN-055	1688	elephant and castle below head					

William & Mary (1688 – 1694)

✓	No.	Date	Features	Grade	Purchased From	Date	Price Paid	Value Now
	WMGN-005	1689						
	WMGN-010	1689	elephant and castle below head					
	WMGN-015	1690						
	WMGN-020	1690	elephant and castle below head					
	WMGN-025	1691						
	WMGN-030	1691	elephant and castle below head					
	WMGN-035	1692						
	WMGN-040	1692	elephant below head					
	WMGN-045	1692	elephant and castle below head					
	WMGN-050	1693						
	WMGN-055	1693	elephant below head					
	WMGN-060	1693	elephant and castle below head					
	WMGN-065	1694						
	WMGN-070	1694	4 over 3					
	WMGN-075	1694	elephant and castle below head					
	WMGN-080	1694	elephant and castle below head; 4 over 3					

William III (1695 – 1701)

✓	No.	Date	Features	Grade	Purchased From	Date	Price Paid	Value Now
	W3GN-005	1695						
	W3GN-010	1695	5 over indeterminate digit					
	W3GN-015	1695	elephant and castle below head					
	W3GN-020	1696						
	W3GN-025	1696	elephant and castle below head					

Cont.

Coincraft's Coin Checklist

✓	No.	Date	Features	Grade	Purchased From	Date	Price Paid	Value Now
	W3GN-030	1697	obv. 1					
	W3GN-035	1697	obv. 2					
	W3GN-040	1697	elephant and castle below head; obv. 2					
	W3GN-045	1698						
	W3GN-050	1698	large date and lettering (rev.)					
	W3GN-055	1698	elephant and castle below head					
	W3GN-060	1699						
	W3GN-065	1699	elephant and castle below head					
	W3GN-070	1700	rev. 2					
	W3GN-075	1700	elephant and castle below head; rev. 2					
	W3GN-080	1700	rev. 3					
	W3GN-085	1700	rev. 4					
	W3GN-090	1701	obv. 2; rev. 5					
	W3GN-095	1701	elephant and castle below head					
	W3GN-100	1701	obv. 2; rev. 6					
	W3GN-105	1701	obv. 2; rev. 7					
	W3GN-110	1701	obv. 3; rev. 5					

Anne (1702 – 1714)

Before Union of England and Scotland

✓	No.	Date	Features	Grade	Purchased From	Date	Price Paid	Value Now
	AGN-005	1702						
	AGN-010	1702	PROOF; edge plain					
	AGN-015	1703	VIGO below head					
	AGN-020	1705						
	AGN-025	1706						
	AGN-030	1707						

After Union of England and Scotland

✓	No.	Date	Features	Grade	Purchased From	Date	Price Paid	Value Now
	AGN-035	1707	obv. 1					
	AGN-040	1707	elephant and castle below head					
	AGN-045	1707	obv. 2					
	AGN-050	1708	obv. 1					
	AGN-055	1708	obv. 2					
	AGN-060	1708	elephant and castle below head					
	AGN-065	1709						
	AGN-070	1709	elephant and castle below head					
	AGN-075	1710						
	AGN-080	1711						
	AGN-085	1712						
	AGN-090	1713						
	AGN-095	1713	3 over 1					
	AGN-100	1714						
	AGN-105	1714	both 'A's in GRATIA unbarred (obv.)					

Guinea

George I (1714 – 1727)

✓	No.	Date	Features	Grade	Purchased From	Date	Price Paid	Value Now
	G1GN-005	1714						
	G1GN-010	1715	obv. 2					
	G1GN-015	1715	obv. 3					
	G1GN-020	1716	obv. 3					
	G1GN-025	1716	obv. 4					
	G1GN-030	1717						
	G1GN-035	1718						
	G1GN-040	1718	8 over 7					
	G1GN-045	1719						
	G1GN-050	1720						
	G1GN-055	1721						
	G1GN-060	1721	elephant and castle below head					
	G1GN-065	1722						
	G1GN-068	1722	latter 2 over 0					
	G1GN-070	1722	elephant and castle below head					
	G1GN-075	1723	obv. 4					
	G1GN-080	1723	obv. 5					
	G1GN-085	1724						
	G1GN-090	1725						
	G1GN-095	1726						
	G1GN-100	1726	elephant and castle below head					
	G1GN-105	1727						

George II (1727 – 1760)

✓	No.	Date	Features	Grade	Purchased From	Date	Price Paid	Value Now
	G2GN-005	1727	obv. 1					
	G2GN-010	1727	obv. 2					
	G2GN-015	1728						
	G2GN-020	1729	PROOF; edge plain					
	G2GN-025	1729	PROOF; edge plain; rev. ↑					
	G2GN-030	1729	E.I.C. below head					
	G2GN-035	1730						
	G2GN-040	1731						
	G2GN-045	1731	E.I.C. below head					
	G2GN-050	1732	obv. 3					
	G2GN-055	1732	E.I.C. below head; obv. 3					
	G2GN-060	1732	obv. 4					
	G2GN-065	1732	E.I.C. below head; obv. 4					
	G2GN-070	1733						
	G2GN-075	1734						
	G2GN-080	1735						
	G2GN-085	1736						
	G2GN-090	1737						
	G2GN-095	1738						
	G2GN-100	1739						
	G2GN-105	1739	E.I.C. below head					

Cont.

Coincraft's Coin Checklist

✓	No.	Date	Features	Grade	Purchased From	Date	Price Paid	Value Now
	G2GN-110	1740						
	G2GN-115	1741	41 over 39					
	G2GN-120	1743						
	G2GN-125	1745						
	G2GN-130	1745	LIMA below head					
	G2GN-135	1746						
	G2GN-140	1747						
	G2GN-145	1748						
	G2GN-150	1749						
	G2GN-155	1750						
	G2GN-160	1751						
	G2GN-165	1752						
	G2GN-170	1753						
	G2GN-175	1755						
	G2GN-180	1756						
	G2GN-185	1758						
	G2GN-190	1759						
	G2GN-195	1760						

George III (1760 – 1820)

✓	No.	Date	Features	Grade	Purchased From	Date	Price Paid	Value Now
	G3GN-005	1761						
	G3GN-010	1761	PROOF; edge plain					
	G3GN-015	1763						
	G3GN-020	1764						
	G3GN-025	1765						
	G3GN-030	1766						
	G3GN-035	1767						
	G3GN-040	1768						
	G3GN-045	1769						
	G3GN-050	1770						
	G3GN-055	1771						
	G3GN-060	1772						
	G3GN-065	1773						
	G3GN-068	1773	3 over 2					
	G3GN-070	1774						
	G3GN-075	1774	PROOF; edge plain; rev. ↑					
	G3GN-080	1775						
	G3GN-085	1776						
	G3GN-090	1777						
	G3GN-095	1778						
	G3GN-100	1779						
	G3GN-105	1781						
	G3GN-110	1782						
	G3GN-115	1783						
	G3GN-120	1784						
	G3GN-125	1785						
	G3GN-130	1786						
	G3GN-135	1787						

Cont.

Guinea

✓	No.	Date	Features	Grade	Purchased From	Date	Price Paid	Value Now
	G3GN-140	1787	PROOF; edge plain					
	G3GN-145	1788						
	G3GN-150	1789						
	G3GN-155	1790						
	G3GN-160	1791						
	G3GN-165	1792						
	G3GN-170	1793						
	G3GN-175	1794						
	G3GN-180	1795						
	G3GN-185	1796						
	G3GN-190	1797						
	G3GN-195	1798						
	G3GN-200	1798	8 over 7					
	G3GN-205	1799						
	G3GN-210	1813						
	G3GN-215	1813	PROOF					

Half Guinea

Charles II   (1660 – 1685)

✓	No.	Date	Features	Grade	Purchased From	Date	Price Paid	Value Now
	C2HGM-005	1669						
	C2HGM-010	1670						
	C2HGM-015	1671						
	C2HGM-020	1672	obv. 1					
	C2HGM-025	1672	obv. 2					
	C2HGM-030	1673						
	C2HGM-035	1674						
	C2HGM-040	1675						
	C2HGM-045	1676						
	C2HGM-050	1676	latter 6 over 4 or 5					
	C2HGM-055	1676	elephant and castle below head					
	C2HGM-060	1677						
	C2HGM-065	1677	elephant and castle below head					
	C2HGM-070	1678						
	C2HGM-075	1678	8 over 7					
	C2HGM-080	1678	elephant and castle below head					
	C2HGM-085	1678	8 over 7 elephant and castle below head					
	C2HGM-090	1679						
	C2HGM-095	1680						
	C2HGM-100	1680	elephant and castle below head					
	C2HGM-105	1681						
	C2HGM-108	1681	elephant and castle below head					
	C2HGM-110	1682						
	C2HGM-115	1682	elephant and castle below head					
	C2HGM-120	1683						
	C2HGM-125	1683	elephant and castle below head					
	C2HGM-130	1684						
	C2HGM-135	1684	elephant and castle below head					

James II   (1685 – 1688)

✓	No.	Date	Features	Grade	Purchased From	Date	Price Paid	Value Now
	J2HG-005	1686						
	J2HG-008	1686	IACOBVS over IACBVS (rev.)					
	J2HG-010	1686	elephant and castle below head					
	J2HG-015	1687						
	J2HG-020	1688						

William & Mary   (1688 – 1694)

✓	No.	Date	Features	Grade	Purchased From	Date	Price Paid	Value Now
	WMHG-005	1689						

Cont.

Half Guinea

✓	No.	Date	Features	Grade	Purchased From	Date	Price Paid	Value Now
	WMHG-010	1690						
	WMHG-015	1691						
	WMHG-020	1691	elephant and castle below head					
	WMHG-025	1692						
	WMHG-030	1692	elephant and castle below head					
	WMHG-035	1692	elephant below head					
	WMHG-040	1693						
	WMHG-045	1693	3 over 2					
	WMHG-050	1694						
	WMHG-055	1694	4 over 3					

William III   (1695 – 1701)

✓	No.	Date	Features	Grade	Purchased From	Date	Price Paid	Value Now
	W3HG-005	1695						
	W3HG-010	1695	elephant and castle below head					
	W3HG-015	1696	elephant and castle below head					
	W3HG-020	1697						
	W3HG-025	1698						
	W3HG-030	1698	elephant and castle below head					
	W3HG-035	1700						
	W3HG-040	1701						

Anne   (1702 – 1714)

✓	No.	Date	Features	Grade	Purchased From	Date	Price Paid	Value Now
	AHG-005	1702						
	AHG-010	1703	VIGO below head					
	AHG-015	1705						
	AHG-020	1707						
	AHG-025	1708						
	AHG-030	1709						
	AHG-035	1710						
	AHG-040	1711						
	AHG-045	1712						
	AHG-050	1713						
	AHG-055	1714						

George I   (1714 – 1727)

✓	No.	Date	Features	Grade	Purchased From	Date	Price Paid	Value Now
	G1HG-005	1715						
	G1HG-010	1717						
	G1HG-015	1718						
	G1HG-020	1718	8 over 7					
	G1HG-022	1718	second 1 over indeterminate digit (8?)					
	G1HG-025	1719						
	G1HG-030	1720						

Cont.

Coincraft's Coin Checklist

✓	No.	Date	Features	Grade	Purchased From	Date	Price Paid	Value Now
	G1HG-035	1721						
	G1HG-040	1721	elephant and castle below head					
	G1HG-045	1722						
	G1HG-050	1722	latter 2 over 0					
	G1HG-055	1723						
	G1HG-060	1724						
	G1HG-065	1725						
	G1HG-070	1726						
	G1HG-075	1727						

George II (1727 – 1760)

✓	No.	Date	Features	Grade	Purchased From	Date	Price Paid	Value Now
	G2HG-005	1728						
	G2HG-010	1728	PROOF; edge plain					
	G2HG-015	1728	PROOF; edge plain; rev. ↑					
	G2HG-020	1729						
	G2HG-025	1729	E.I.C. below head					
	G2HG-030	1730						
	G2HG-035	1730	E.I.C. below head					
	G2HG-040	1731						
	G2HG-045	1731	E.I.C. below head					
	G2HG-050	1732						
	G2HG-055	1732	E.I.C. below head					
	G2HG-060	1734						
	G2HG-065	1736						
	G2HG-070	1737						
	G2HG-075	1738						
	G2HG-080	1739						
	G2HG-085	1739	E.I.C. below head					
	G2HG-090	1740						
	G2HG-095	1743						
	G2HG-100	1745						
	G2HG-105	1745	LIMA below head					
	G2HG-110	1746						
	G2HG-115	1747						
	G2HG-120	1748						
	G2HG-125	1749						
	G2HG-130	1750						
	G2HG-135	1751						
	G2HG-140	1751	latter 1 over 0					
	G2HG-145	1752						
	G2HG-150	1753						
	G2HG-155	1755						
	G2HG-160	1756						
	G2HG-165	1758						
	G2HG-170	1759						
	G2HG-175	1759	9 over 8					
	G2HG-180	1760						

Half Guinea

George III (1760 – 1820)

✓	No.	Date	Features	Grade	Purchased From	Date	Price Paid	Value Now
	G3HG-005	1762						
	G3HG-010	1763						
	G3HG-015	1764						
	G3HG-020	1765						
	G3HG-025	1765	5 over 4					
	G3HG-030	1766						
	G3HG-035	1768						
	G3HG-040	1769						
	G3HG-045	1772						
	G3HG-050	1773						
	G3HG-055	1774	obv. 2					
	G3HG-060	1774	obv. 3					
	G3HG-065	1775	obv. 2					
	G3HG-070	1775	obv. 3					
	G3HG-075	1775	PROOF; edge plain; obv. 3					
	G3HG-080	1775	obv. 4					
	G3HG-085	1776						
	G3HG-090	1777						
	G3HG-095	1778						
	G3HG-100	1779						
	G3HG-105	1781						
	G3HG-110	1783						
	G3HG-115	1784						
	G3HG-120	1785						
	G3HG-125	1786						
	G3HG-130	1787						
	G3HG-135	1787	PROOF; edge plain					
	G3HG-140	1787	PROOF in silver; edge plain					
	G3HG-145	1788						
	G3HG-150	1789						
	G3HG-155	1790						
	G3HG-160	1791						
	G3HG-165	1792						
	G3HG-170	1793						
	G3HG-175	1794						
	G3HG-180	1795						
	G3HG-185	1796						
	G3HG-190	1797						
	G3HG-195	1798						
	G3HG-200	1798	8 over 7					
	G3HG-205	1800						
	G3HG-210	1801						
	G3HG-215	1802						
	G3HG-220	1803						
	G3HG-225	1804						
	G3HG-230	1805						
	G3HG-235	1806						
	G3HG-240	1808						

Cont.

Coincraft's Coin Checklist

✓	No.	Date	Features	Grade	Purchased From	Date	Price Paid	Value Now
	G3HG-245	1809						
	G3HG-250	1810						
	G3HG-255	1811						
	G3HG-260	1813						

Third Guinea

George III (1760 – 1820)

✓	No.	Date	Features	Grade	Purchased From	Date	Price Paid	Value Now
	G3TG-005	1797						
	G3TG-010	1798						
	G3TG-015	1799						
	G3TG-020	1800						
	G3TG-025	1801						
	G3TG-030	1802						
	G3TG-035	1803						
	G3TG-040	1804						
	G3TG-045	1806						
	G3TG-050	1808						
	G3TG-055	1809						
	G3TG-060	1810						
	G3TG-065	1811						
	G3TG-070	1813						
	G3TG-075	1813	PROOF					

Quarter Guinea

George I (1714 – 1727)

✓	No.	Date	Features	Grade	Purchased From	Date	Price Paid	Value Now
	G1QG-005	1718	obv. 1					
	G1QG-010	1718	obv. 2					

George III (1760 – 1820)

✓	No.	Date	Features	Grade	Purchased From	Date	Price Paid	Value Now
	G3QG-005	1762						

Crown

Oliver Cromwell (Commonwealth 1649 – 1660)

✓	No.	Date	Features	Grade	Purchased From	Date	Price Paid	Value Now
	CRCR-005	1658	8 over 7					
	CRCR-010	1658	struck in gold; 8 over 7					

Charles II (1660 – 1685)

✓	No.	Date	Features	Grade	Purchased From	Date	Price Paid	Value Now
	C2CRM-005	1662	obv. 1; edge DECVS ET TVTAMEN					
	C2CRM-010	1662	PROOF; edge as above					
	C2CRM-015	1662	rev. ↑; edge as above					
	C2CRM-020	1662	obv. 1; regnal edge 1662					
	C2CRM-025	1662	obv. 2; edge DECVS ET TVTAMEN					
	C2CRM-030	1662	rev. ↑; edge as above					
	C2CRM-035	1662	PROOF; edge plain					
	C2CRM-040	1662	obv. 2; regnal edge 1662					
	C2CRM-045	1663	regnal edge XV					
	C2CRM-050	1663	no stops rev.					
	C2CRM-055	1663	no edge date					
	C2CRM-060	1663	PROOF					
	C2CRM-065	1663	PROOF in gold					
	C2CRM-070	1664						
	C2CRM-075	1664	PROOF					
	C2CRM-080	1665	regnal edge XVI					
	C2CRM-085	1665	regnal edge XVII					
	C2CRM-090	1665	5 over 4; regnal edge XVII					
	C2CRM-095	1666						
	C2CRM-100	1666	ANN instead of ANNO (edge)					
	C2CRM-105	1666	RE.X instead of REX (rev.)					
	C2CRM-110	1666	elephant below head					
	C2CRM-115	1666	elephant below head; reads RE.X on rev.					
	C2CRM-120	1667	regnal edge XVIII					
	C2CRM-125	1667	regnal edge DECIMO NONO					
	C2CRM-130	1668						
	C2CRM-135	1668	DECVS ET TVTAMEN inverted relative to rest of inscription (edge)					
	C2CRM-138	1668	8 over 5					
	C2CRM-140	1668	8 over 7					
	C2CRM-145	1669						
	C2CRM-150	1669	9 over 8					
	C2CRM-155	1670						
	C2CRM-160	1670	70 over 69					
	C2CRM-165	1671	regnal edge VICESIMO TERTIO					

Cont.

Coincraft's Coin Checklist

✓	No.	Date	Features	Grade	Purchased From	Date	Price Paid	Value Now
	C2CRM-170	1671	T of ET over R (rev.); regnal edge as above					
	C2CRM-175	1671	ET over FR (rev.); regnal edge as above					
	C2CRM-180	1671	regnal edge as above					
	C2CRM-185	1671	regnal edge VICESIMO QVARTO					
	C2CRM-190	1672						
	C2CRM-195	1673	regnal edge VICESIMO QVARTO					
	C2CRM-200	1673	regnal edge VICESIMO QVINTO					
	C2CRM-205	1673	3 over 2; regnal edge as above					
	C2CRM-210	1674						
	C2CRM-215	1675						
	C2CRM-220	1675	EGNI instead of REGNI (edge)					
	C2CRM-225	1675	5 over 3					
	C2CRM-230	1676						
	C2CRM-235	1676	EGNI instead of REGNI (edge)					
	C2CRM-240	1677						
	C2CRM-245	1677	7 over 6					
	C2CRM-250	1678	8 over 7					
	C2CRM-255	1679	obv. 4					
	C2CRM-260	1679	obv. 5					
	C2CRM-265	1679	obv. 5; reads HIBR.EX (rev.)					
	C2CRM-270	1680	obv. 4					
	C2CRM-275	1680	obv. 4; 80 over 79					
	C2CRM-280	1680	obv. 5					
	C2CRM-285	1680	obv. 5; 80 over 79					
	C2CRM-290	1681						
	C2CRM-295	1681	elephant and castle below head					
	C2CRM-300	1682						
	C2CRM-305	1682	2 over 1					
	C2CRM-310	1682	QVARTO appears to read QVRRTO (edge)					
	C2CRM-315	1682	2 over 1; QVARTO appears to read QVRRTO (edge)					
	C2CRM-320	1683						
	C2CRM-325	1684						

James II (1685 – 1688)

✓	No.	Date	Features	Grade	Purchased From	Date	Price Paid	Value Now
	J2CR-005	1686						
	J2CR-010	1686	no stops on obv.					
	J2CR-015	1687						
	J2CR-020	1687	struck on 41mm diameter flan					
	J2CR-025	1688						
	J2CR-030	1688	A in IACOBVS and latter A in GRATIA unbarred					
	J2CR-035	1688	8 over 7					

William & Mary (1688 – 1694)

✓	No.	Date	Features	Grade	Purchased From	Date	Price Paid	Value Now
	WMCR-005	1691						
	WMCR-010	1691	TERTTIO instead of TERTIO (edge)					
	WMCR-015	1692						
	WMCR-020	1692	2 over inverted 2; regnal edge QVARTO					
	WMCR-025	1692	2 over inverted 2; regnal edge QVINTO					

William III (1695 – 1701)

✓	No.	Date	Features	Grade	Purchased From	Date	Price Paid	Value Now
	W3CR-005	1695	regnal edge SEPTIMO					
	W3CR-010	1695	regnal edge OCTAVO					
	W3CR-015	1695	regnal edge OCAVO (error)					
	W3CR-020	1695	PROOF; edge plain					
	W3CR-025	1696	obv. 1					
	W3CR-030	1696	NNO instead of ANNO (edge)					
	W3CR-035	1696	regnal edge OCAVO (error)					
	W3CR-040	1696	PROOF; edge plain					
	W3CR-045	1696	PROOF; edge plain; rev. ↑					
	W3CR-050	1696	6 over 5					
	W3CR-055	1696	6 over 9 or inverted 6					
	W3CR-060	1696	no stops in obv. legend					
	W3CR-065	1696	G of GRA over D (obv.)					
	W3CR-070	1696	GEI instead of DEI (obv.)					
	W3CR-072	1696	GEI instead of DEI (obv.); G of GRA over F (obv.)					
	W3CR-075	1696	regnal edge OCTAVO; obv. 2					
	W3CR-080	1696	no stops in rev. legend					
	W3CR-085	1696	edge lettering blundered					
	W3CR-090	1696	regnal edge TRICESIMO; obv. 2					
	W3CR-095	1697						
	W3CR-100	1700	regnal edge DVODECIMO					
	W3CR-105	1700	regnal edge DECIMO TERTIO					
	W3CR-110	1700	D over inverted D in DECIMO TERTIO (edge)					

Anne (1702 – 1714)

Before Union of England and Scotland

✓	No.	Date	Features	Grade	Purchased From	Date	Price Paid	Value Now
	ACR-005	1703	VIGO below head					
	ACR-010	1705	plumes on rev.					
	ACR-015	1706	roses and plumes on rev.					

Cont.

Coincraft's Coin Checklist

✓	No.	Date	Features	Grade	Purchased From	Date	Price Paid	Value Now
	ACR-020	1707	roses and plumes on rev.					

After Union of England and Scotland

✓	No.	Date	Features	Grade	Purchased From	Date	Price Paid	Value Now
	ACR-025	1707	E below head; regnal edge SEXTO					
	ACR-030	1707	E below head; regnal edge SEPTIMO					
	ACR-035	1707	plain below head					
	ACR-040	1708						
	ACR-045	1708	plumes on rev.; rev. 2					
	ACR-050	1708	plumes on rev.; rev. 3					
	ACR-055	1708	E below head					
	ACR-060	1708	8 over 7 E below head					
	ACR-065	1713	roses and plumes on rev.					
	ACR-070	1713	roses and plumes on rev.; regnal edge DVODECIM (error)					

George I (1714 – 1727)

✓	No.	Date	Features	Grade	Purchased From	Date	Price Paid	Value Now
	G1CR-005	1716	roses and plumes on rev.					
	G1CR-010	1718	roses and plumes on rev.					
	G1CR-015	1718	8 over 6 roses and plumes on rev.					
	G1CR-020	1720	roses and plumes on rev.					
	G1CR-025	1720	20 over 18 roses and plumes on rev.					
	G1CR-030	1723	SSC on rev.					
	G1CR-035	1726	roses and plumes on rev.					
	G1CR-040	1726	roses and plumes on rev.; each N on edge inverted (top left of N has no serif)					

George II (1727 – 1760)

✓	No.	Date	Features	Grade	Purchased From	Date	Price Paid	Value Now
	G2CR-010	1732	roses and plumes on rev.					
	G2CR-015	1732	roses and plumes on rev. PROOF; edge plain					
	G2CR-020	1734	roses and plumes on rev.					
	G2CR-025	1734	roses and plumes on rev.; edge reads DEC...AME ...NNO REGNI					
	G2CR-030	1735	roses and plumes on rev.					
	G2CR-035	1735	roses and plumes on rev.; each 'E' on edge is over a 'B'					
	G2CR-040	1735	T of OCTAVO over V (edge)					
	G2CR-045	1736	roses and plumes on rev.					
	G2CR-050	1739	roses on rev.					
	G2CR-055	1741	roses on rev.					
	G2CR-060	1743	roses on rev.					
	G2CR-065	1746	LIMA below head					
	G2CR-070	1746	PROOF					
	G2CR-075	1750						
	G2CR-080	1751						

Crown

George III (1760 – 1820)

✓	No.	Date	Features	Grade	Purchased From	Date	Price Paid	Value Now
	G3CR-005	none	obv. 1; rev. 1					
	G3CR-010	none	obv. 2; rev. 2					
	G3CR-015	none	obv. 3; rev. 3					
	G3CR-020	none	obv. 4; rev. 4					
	G3CR-025	none	obv. 5; rev. 5					
	G3CR-030	none	obv. 6; rev. 6					
	G3CR-035	none	obv. 7; rev. 7					
	G3CR-040	none	obv. 8; rev. 8					
	G3CR-045	none	obv. 9; rev. 9					
	G3CR-050	none	obv. 10; rev. 10					
	G3CR-055	none	obv. 11; rev. 11					
	G3CR-060	none	obv. 12; rev. 12					
	G3CR-065	none	obv. 13; rev. 13					
	G3CR-070	none	obv. 14; rev. 14					
	G3CR-075	none	obv. 15; rev. 15					
	G3CR-078	none	obv. 16; rev. 16					

Bank of England Dollar

✓	No.	Date	Features	Grade	Purchased From	Date	Price Paid	Value Now
	G3CR-080	1804	obv. 1; rev. 1					
	G3CR-085	1804	PROOF; obv. 1; rev. 1					
	G3CR-090	1804	PROOF in copper; obv. 1; rev. 1					
	G3CR-095	1804	obv. 1; rev. 3					
	G3CR-100	1804	obv. 2; rev. 1					
	G3CR-105	1804	PROOF; obv. 2; rev. 1					
	G3CR-110	1804	obv. 3; rev. 1					
	G3CR-115	1804	PROOF; obv. 3; rev. 1					
	G3CR-120	1804	PROOF in silver gilt; obv. 3; rev. 1					
	G3CR-125	1804	PROOF in copper; obv. 3; rev. 1					
	G3CR-130	1804	obv. 3; rev. 2					
	G3CR-135	1804	PROOF; obv. 3; rev. 2					
	G3CR-140	1804	PROOF in copper; obv. 3; rev. 2					
	G3CR-145	1804	obv. 3; rev. 3					
	G3CR-150	1804	PROOF in copper; obv. 3; rev. 3					
	G3CR-155	1804	obv. 4; rev. 1					
	G3CR-160	1804	PROOF; obv. 4; rev. 1					
	G3CR-165	1804	PROOF in copper; rev. ↓; obv. 4; rev. 1					
	G3CR-170	1804	obv. 5; rev. 1					
	G3CR-175	1804	obv. 5; rev. 2					
	G3CR-180	1804	PROOF; obv. 5; rev. 2					
	G3CR-185	1804	PROOF in copper; obv. 5; rev. 2					
	G3CR-190	1804	obv. 5; rev. 3					
	G3CR-195	1804	PROOF in copper; obv. 5; rev. 3					

Double Florin

Victoria   (1837 – 1901)

✓	No.	Date	Features	Grade	Purchased From	Date	Price Paid	Value Now
	VJDFL-005	1887	Roman I in date					
	VJDFL-010	1887	PROOF Roman I in date					
	VJDFL-015	1887	Arabic 1 in date; obv. 1					
	VJDFL-020	1887	Arabic 1 in date; obv. 2					
	VJDFL-025	1887	PROOF Arabic 1 in date					
	VJDFL-030	1888						
	VJDFL-035	1888	second I in VICTORIA is inverted '1'					
	VJDFL-040	1889						
	VJDFL-045	1889	second I in VICTORIA is inverted '1'					
	VJDFL-050	1890						

Three Shillings

George III (1760 – 1820)

✓	No.	Date	Features	Grade	Purchased From	Date	Price Paid	Value Now
	G33S-005	1811						
	G33S-010	1811	PROOF					
	G33S-015	1812	obv. 1; rev. 1					
	G33S-020	1812	obv. 2; rev. 2					
	G33S-025	1812	PROOF; obv. 2; rev. 2					
	G33S-030	1812	PROOF in gold; obv. 2; rev. 2					
	G33S-035	1812	PROOF in platinum; obv. 2; rev. 2					
	G33S-040	1813						
	G33S-045	1814						
	G33S-050	1815						
	G33S-055	1816						

Halfcrown

Oliver Cromwell (Commonwealth 1649 – 1660)

✓	No.	Date	Features	Grade	Purchased From	Date	Price Paid	Value Now
	CRHC-005	1656						
	CRHC-010	1658						
	CRHC-015	1658	PROOF in gold					

Charles II (1660 – 1685)

✓	No.	Date	Features	Grade	Purchased From	Date	Price Paid	Value Now
	C2HCM-005	1663						
	C2HCM-010	1663	rev. ↑					
	C2HCM-015	1663	rev. 90 degrees anticlockwise					
	C2HCM-020	1663	no stops on obv.					
	C2HCM-025	1663	no stops on obv.; R of FRA over B (rev.)					
	C2HCM-030	1663	V of CAROLVS over S (obv.)					
	C2HCM-035	1663	no stops on obv. and V of CAROLVS over S (obv.)					
	C2HCM-040	1663	PROOF					
	C2HCM-045	1664						
	C2HCM-050	1666	last 6 over indeterminate digit					
	C2HCM-055	1666	last 6 over 4 elephant below head					
	C2HCM-060	1666	last 6 over indeterminate digit elephant below head					
	C2HCM-065	1667	7 over 4					
	C2HCM-070	1668	8 over 4					
	C2HCM-072	1668	8 over 4: CAROL∀S instead of CAROLVS (obv.)					
	C2HCM-075	1669						
	C2HCM-080	1669	R of PRIMO over I (edge)					
	C2HCM-085	1669	9 over 4					
	C2HCM-090	1670						
	C2HCM-092	1670	V of CAROLVS over S (obv.)					
	C2HCM-095	1670	MRG instead of MAG (rev.)					
	C2HCM-100	1670	A of MAG over R (rev.)					
	C2HCM-102	1670	E of ET over R (rev.)					
	C2HCM-105	1671						
	C2HCM-110	1671	A of MAG over R (rev.)					
	C2HCM-115	1671	1 over 0					
	C2HCM-120	1672	edge VICESIMO TERTIO; obv. 4					
	C2HCM-125	1672	edge VICESIMO QVARTO; obv. 4					
	C2HCM-130	1672	edge VICESIMO QVARTO; obv. 5					
	C2HCM-135	1673						
	C2HCM-140	1673	B of BR over R (rev.)					
	C2HCM-145	1673	A of FRA over R (rev.)					
	C2HCM-150	1673	EGNI instead of REGNI (edge)					

Cont.

Halfcrown

✓	No.	Date	Features	Grade	Purchased From	Date	Price Paid	Value Now
	C2HCM-155	1673	plume below head					
	C2HCM-160	1673	plume below head and in centre of rev.					
	C2HCM-165	1674						
	C2HCM-170	1674	4 over 3					
	C2HCM-175	1675						
	C2HCM-180	1675	EGNI instead of REGNI (edge)					
	C2HCM-185	1675	reversed 1 in date					
	C2HCM-190	1676						
	C2HCM-195	1676	EGNI instead of REGNI (edge)					
	C2HCM-198	1676	R of BR over I (rev.)					
	C2HCM-200	1676	reversed 1 in date					
	C2HCM-202	1676	reversed 1 in date; F of FRA over H; R of BR over T					
	C2HCM-205	1677						
	C2HCM-210	1678						
	C2HCM-212	1678	RRGNI or RBGNI instead of REGNI (edge)					
	C2HCM-215	1679						
	C2HCM-218	1679	REG instead of REGNI (edge)					
	C2HCM-220	1679	GRATTA instead of GRATIA (obv.)					
	C2HCM-225	1679	DECNS instead of DECVS (edge)					
	C2HCM-230	1679	DNCVS instead of DECVS (edge)					
	C2HCM-235	1679	both 'V's on edge are inverted 'A's					
	C2HCM-240	1679	N in REGNI is inverted R (edge)					
	C2HCM-245	1679	PRICESIMO instead of TRICESIMO (edge)					
	C2HCM-250	1680						
	C2HCM-252	1680	H of HIB unbarred (rev.)					
	C2HCM-255	1680	RGNI instead of REGNI (edge)					
	C2HCM-258	1680	DECV instead of DECVS (edge)					
	C2HCM-260	1680	D in SECVNDO inverted (edge)					
	C2HCM-265	1681						
	C2HCM-270	1681	1 over 0					
	C2HCM-275	1681	elephant and castle below head					
	C2HCM-280	1682						
	C2HCM-285	1682	PROOF (?) rev. ↑					
	C2HCM-290	1682	2 over 1					
	C2HCM-295	1682	82 over 79					
	C2HCM-300	1683						
	C2HCM-305	1683	plume below head					
	C2HCM-310	1684	4 over 3					

James II (1685 – 1688)

✓	No.	Date	Features	Grade	Purchased From	Date	Price Paid	Value Now
	J2HC-005	1685						
	J2HC-010	1686	edge SECVNDO					
	J2HC-015	1686	6 over 5; edge SECVNDO					
	J2HC-020	1686	edge TERTIO					

Cont.

Coincraft's Coin Checklist

✓	No.	Date	Features	Grade	Purchased From	Date	Price Paid	Value Now
	J2HC-025	1686	V of IACOBVS over B (obv.); edge TERTIO					
	J2HC-030	1686	V of IACOBVS over S (obv.); edge TERTIO					
	J2HC-032	1686	IACOB∇S instead of IACOBVS (obv.); edge TERTIO					
	J2HC-035	1687	obv. 1					
	J2HC-040	1687	7 over 6; obv. 1					
	J2HC-045	1687	6 over 8; obv. 1					
	J2HC-050	1687	obv. 2					
	J2HC-055	1687	PROOF; obv. 2					
	J2HC-060	1688						

William & Mary (1688 – 1694)

✓	No.	Date	Features	Grade	Purchased From	Date	Price Paid	Value Now
	WMHC-005	1689	rev. 1					
	WMHC-010	1689	FRA instead of FR (rev.); rev. 1					
	WMHC-015	1689	second L of GVLIELMVS over M (obv.); rev. 1					
	WMHC-020	1689	first V of GVLIELMVS over A (obv.); rev. 1					
	WMHC-022	1689	DECV instead of DECVS (edge); rev. 1					
	WMHC-025	1689	no stops on obv.; rev. 1					
	WMHC-030	1689	rev. 2					
	WMHC-035	1690						
	WMHC-040	1690	GRETIA instead of GRATIA; second V of GVLIELMVS over S (obv.)					
	WMHC-045	1690						
	WMHC-050	1691						
	WMHC-055	1692	edge QVARTO					
	WMHC-060	1692	edge QVINTO					
	WMHC-065	1693						
	WMHC-070	1693	3 over inverted 3					
	WMHC-075	1693	3 of date inverted					

William III (1695 – 1701)

✓	No.	Date	Features	Grade	Purchased From	Date	Price Paid	Value Now
	W3HC-005	1696	rev. 1					
	W3HC-010	1696	mintmark B; rev. 1					
	W3HC-015	1696	mintmark B; PROOF; rev. 1					
	W3HC-020	1696	mintmark C; rev. 1					
	W3HC-025	1696	mintmark E; rev. 1					
	W3HC-030	1696	mintmark E; DECVS AMEN AMEN instead of DECVS ET TVTAMEN (edge); rev. 1					
	W3HC-035	1696	mintmark N; rev. 1					
	W3HC-040	1696	mintmark y; rev. 1					
	W3HC-045	1696	rev. 2					
	W3HC-050	1696	PROOF on thick flan; edge plain; rev. 2					

Cont.

Halfcrown

✓	No.	Date	Features	Grade	Purchased From	Date	Price Paid	Value Now
	W3HC-055	1696	mintmark B; rev. 2					
	W3HC-060	1696	mintmark B; struck on thick flan; rev. 2					
	W3HC-065	1696	mintmark C; rev. 2					
	W3HC-070	1696	mintmark E; rev. 2					
	W3HC-075	1696	E over B (mintmark); rev. 2					
	W3HC-080	1696	mintmark N; rev. 2					
	W3HC-085	1696	mintmark y; rev. 2					
	W3HC-090	1696	y over E (mintmark); rev. 2					
	W3HC-095	1696	mintmark y; arms of Scotland at date; rev. 2					
	W3HC-100	1696	rev. 3					
	W3HC-105	1696	mintmark C; rev. 3					
	W3HC-110	1696	mintmark E; edge OCTAVO; rev. 3					
	W3HC-115	1696	mintmark E; edge NONO; rev. 3					
	W3HC-120	1696	mintmark N; rev. 3					
	W3HC-125	1697						
	W3HC-130	1697	7 over 6					
	W3HC-135	1697	GRR instead of GRA (obv.)					
	W3HC-138	1697	GR∧ instead of GRA (obv.)					
	W3HC-140	1697	GVLIEIMVS instead of GVLIELMVS (obv.)					
	W3HC-142	1697	DEC∀S ET T∀TAMEN instead of DECVS ET TVTAMEN (edge)					
	W3HC-145	1697	PROOF; edge plain					
	W3HC-150	1697	mintmark B					
	W3HC-155	1697	mintmark B; no stops on rev.					
	W3HC-160	1697	mintmark B; no harp strings					
	W3HC-165	1697	mintmark B; PROOF on thick flan					
	W3HC-170	1697	mintmark C					
	W3HC-175	1697	mintmark C; no harp strings					
	W3HC-180	1697	mintmark E					
	W3HC-185	1697	mintmark E; T∀TAMEN instead of TVTAMEN (edge)					
	W3HC-190	1697	mintmark E; E over C (mintmark)					
	W3HC-195	1697	mintmark E; E over B (mintmark)					
	W3HC-200	1697	mintmark E; error edge OCTAVO					
	W3HC-205	1697	mintmark N					
	W3HC-210	1697	mintmark N; arms of Scotland at date					
	W3HC-215	1697	mintmark N; error edge OCTAVO					
	W3HC-220	1697	mintmark y					
	W3HC-225	1697	mintmark y; no harp strings					
	W3HC-230	1697	mintmark y; error edge OCTAVO					
	W3HC-235	1698	edge DECIMO					
	W3HC-240	1698	edge DECIMO; 8 over 7					
	W3HC-245	1698	edge DECIMO; GR∧ instead of GRA (obv.)					
	W3HC-250	1698	edge DECIMO; GVLIEIMVS instead of GVLIELMVS (obv.)					
	W3HC-255	1698	edge UNDECIMO					
	W3HC-260	1698	error edge OCTAVO					
	W3HC-265	1699						

Cont.

Coincraft's Coin Checklist

√	No.	Date	Features	Grade	Purchased From	Date	Price Paid	Value Now
	W3HC-270	1699	T∀TAMEN instead of TVTAMEN (edge)					
	W3HC-275	1699	DEC∀S ET T∀TAMEN instead of DECVS ET TVTAMEN					
	W3HC-280	1699	arms of Scotland at date					
	W3HC-285	1699	central lion inverted (rev.)					
	W3HC-290	1700	edge DVODECIMO					
	W3HC-295	1700	edge DECIMO TERTIO					
	W3HC-300	1700	edge DECIMO TERTIO; DEC∀S instead of DECVS (edge)					
	W3HC-305	1701						
	W3HC-310	1701	no stops on rev.					
	W3HC-315	1701	elephant and castle below head					
	W3HC-320	1701	plumes on rev.					

Anne (1702 – 1714)

Before Union of England and Scotland

√	No.	Date	Features	Grade	Purchased From	Date	Price Paid	Value Now
	AHC-005	1703	VIGO below head					
	AHC-010	1703						
	AHC-015	1704	plumes on rev.					
	AHC-020	1705	plumes on rev.					
	AHC-025	1706	roses and plumes on rev.					
	AHC-028	1706	T of QVINTO over V (edge)					
	AHC-030	1707	roses and plumes on rev.					

After Union of England and Scotland

√	No.	Date	Features	Grade	Purchased From	Date	Price Paid	Value Now
	AHC-035	1707	E below head; edge SEXTO					
	AHC-040	1707	E below head; ET*T*TAMEN instead of ET TVTAMEN; edge SEXTO					
	AHC-045	1707	E below head; edge SEPTIMO					
	AHC-050	1707	edge SEPTIMO					
	AHC-055	1707	ET.T.TVTAMEN instead of ET TVTAMEN (edge); edge SEPTIMO					
	AHC-060	1707	struck on thick flan; edge SEPTIMO					
	AHC-065	1708	E below head					
	AHC-070	1708						
	AHC-075	1708	plumes on rev.					
	AHC-080	1709						
	AHC-085	1709	E below head; rev. ↑					
	AHC-090	1710	roses and plumes on rev.					
	AHC-095	1712	roses and plumes on rev.					
	AHC-098	1712	roses and plumes on rev.; DEC∀S instead of DECVS (edge)					
	AHC-100	1713						
	AHC-105	1713	roses and plumes on rev.					
	AHC-108	1713	roses and plumes on rev.; DEC∀S ET T∀TAMEN instead of DECVS ET TVTAMEN (edge)					
	AHC-110	1714	roses and plumes on rev.					

Cont.

Halfcrown

✓	No.	Date	Features	Grade	Purchased From	Date	Price Paid	Value Now
	AHC-115	1714	roses and plumes on rev.; ANN instead of ANNO (edge)					
	AHC-120	1714	4 over 3 roses and plumes on rev.					

George I (1714 – 1727)

✓	No.	Date	Features	Grade	Purchased From	Date	Price Paid	Value Now
	G1HC-005	1715	PROOF or PATTERN; edge plain					
	G1HC-010	1715	roses and plumes on rev.					
	G1HC-012	1715	roses and plumes on rev.; NNO instead of ANNO (edge)					
	G1HC-015	1715	roses and plumes on rev.; edge lettering blundered					
	G1HC-020	1715	roses and plumes on rev.; edge plain					
	G1HC-025	1717	roses and plumes on rev.					
	G1HC-030	1720	roses and plumes on rev.					
	G1HC-035	1720	20 over 17 roses and plumes on rev.					
	G1HC-040	1723	SSC on rev.					
	G1HC-045	1726	roses and plumes on rev.					

George II (1727 – 1760)

✓	No.	Date	Features	Grade	Purchased From	Date	Price Paid	Value Now
	G2HC-005	1731	PROOF or PATTERN; edge plain					
	G2HC-010	1731	roses and plumes on rev.					
	G2HC-015	1732	roses and plumes on rev.					
	G2HC-020	1734	roses and plumes on rev.					
	G2HC-025	1735	roses and plumes on rev.					
	G2HC-030	1736	roses and plumes on rev.					
	G2HC-035	1739	roses on rev.					
	G2HC-038	1739	roses on rev.; TVTAME instead of TVTAMEN (edge)					
	G2HC-040	1741	roses on rev.					
	G2HC-045	1741	41 over 39 roses on rev.					
	G2HC-050	1743	roses on rev.					
	G2HC-055	1745	roses on rev.					
	G2HC-060	1745	5 over 3 roses on rev.					
	G2HC-065	1745	LIMA below head					
	G2HC-070	1746	LIMA below head					
	G2HC-075	1746	6 over 5 LIMA below head					
	G2HC-080	1746	PROOF					
	G2HC-082	1746	PROOF; E of DECVS over A					
	G2HC-085	1750						
	G2HC-090	1751						

George III (1760 – 1820)

✓	No.	Date	Features	Grade	Purchased From	Date	Price Paid	Value Now
	G3HC-005	none	obv. 1; rev. 1					

Cont.

Coincraft's Coin Checklist

✓	No.	Date	Features	Grade	Purchased From	Date	Price Paid	Value Now
	G3HC-010	none	obv. 2; rev. 2					
	G3HC-015	none	obv. 3; rev. 3					
	G3HC-020	none	obv. 4; rev. 4					
	G3HC-025	none	obv. 5; rev. 5					
	G3HC-030	none	obv. 6; rev. 6					

Eighteen Pence Bank Token

George III (1760 – 1820)

✓	No.	Date	Features	Grade	Purchased From	Date	Price Paid	Value Now
	G318D-005	1811						
	G318D-010	1811	PROOF					
	G318D-015	1812	obv. 1					
	G318D-020	1812	obv. 2					
	G318D-025	1812	PROOF; obv. 2					
	G318D-030	1812	PROOF; small lettering on rev.; obv. 2					
	G318D-035	1812	PROOF in platinum; obv. 2					
	G318D-040	1813						
	G318D-045	1813	PROOF in platinum					
	G318D-050	1814						
	G318D-055	1815						
	G318D-060	1816						

Shilling

Oliver Cromwell (Commonwealth 1649 – 1660)

✓	No.	Date	Features	Grade	Purchased From	Date	Price Paid	Value Now
	CRSH-005	1658						

Charles II (1660 – 1685)

✓	No.	Date	Features	Grade	Purchased From	Date	Price Paid	Value Now
	C2SHM-005	1663	obv. 1					
	C2SHM-010	1663	rev. ↑					
	C2SHM-015	1663	GARTIA instead of GRATIA (obv.)					
	C2SHM-020	1663	Scotland/Ireland shields transposed					
	C2SHM-025	1663	A of FRA over G (rev.)					
	C2SHM-030	1663	PROOF in copper; edge plain					
	C2SHM-035	1663	obv. 2					
	C2SHM-040	1666	obv. 2					
	C2SHM-045	1666	elephant below head; obv. 2					
	C2SHM-050	1666	elephant below 'guinea' head					
	C2SHM-055	1666	obv. 4					
	C2SHM-060	1668	obv. 2					
	C2SHM-065	1668	obv. 4					
	C2SHM-070	1668	8 over 3 (?); obv. 4					
	C2SHM-075	1669	9 over 6 (?); obv. 2					
	C2SHM-080	1669	obv. 4					
	W3SH-035	1669	head of William III (error date)					
	C2SHM-085	1670						
	C2SHM-090	1671						
	C2SHM-095	1671	plume both sides					
	C2SHM-100	1672						
	C2SHM-105	1672	2 over 1					
	C2SHM-110	1673						
	C2SHM-115	1673	3 over 2					
	C2SHM-118	1673	E of ET over R (rev.)					
	C2SHM-120	1673	plume both sides					
	C2SHM-125	1674	obv. 4					
	C2SHM-130	1674	4 over 3					
	C2SHM-135	1674	plume both sides					
	C2SHM-140	1674	plume on rev.					
	C2SHM-145	1674	obv. 5					
	C2SHM-150	1675	obv. 5					
	C2SHM-155	1675	5 over 3; obv. 5					
	C2SHM-160	1675	obv. 4					
	C2SHM-165	1675	5 over 4; obv. 4					
	C2SHM-170	1675	plume both sides					
	C2SHM-172	1675	plume both sides; 5 over 3					
	C2SHM-175	1676						

Cont.

Shilling

✓	No.	Date	Features	Grade	Purchased From	Date	Price Paid	Value Now
	C2SHM-180	1676	6 over 5					
	C2SHM-185	1676	plume both sides					
	C2SHM-190	1677						
	C2SHM-195	1677	plume below head					
	C2SHM-200	1678						
	C2SHM-205	1678	8 over 7					
	C2SHM-210	1679						
	C2SHM-215	1679	9 over 7					
	C2SHM-220	1679	plume both sides					
	C2SHM-225	1679	plume below head					
	C2SHM-230	1680						
	C2SHM-235	1680	80 over 79					
	C2SHM-240	1680	plume both sides					
	C2SHM-245	1681						
	C2SHM-250	1681	1 over 0					
	C2SHM-255	1681	1 over 0 elephant and castle					
	C2SHM-260	1682	2 over 1					
	C2SHM-265	1683	obv. 4					
	C2SHM-270	1683	obv. 6					
	C2SHM-275	1684						

James II   (1685 – 1688)

✓	No.	Date	Features	Grade	Purchased From	Date	Price Paid	Value Now
	J2SH-005	1685						
	J2SH-010	1685	no stops on rev.					
	J2SH-015	1685	plume on rev.					
	J2SH-020	1686						
	J2SH-025	1686	latter 6 over 5					
	J2SH-030	1686	V of IACOBVS over S (obv.)					
	J2SH-035	1686	G of MAG over A (rev.)					
	J2SH-040	1687						
	J2SH-045	1687	7 over 6					
	J2SH-050	1687	7 over 6 G of MAG over A (rev.)					
	J2SH-055	1688						
	J2SH-060	1688	latter 8 over 7					

William & Mary   (1688 – 1694)

✓	No.	Date	Features	Grade	Purchased From	Date	Price Paid	Value Now
	WMSH-005	1692						
	WMSH-010	1692	inverted 1 in date					
	WMSH-015	1693						
	WMSH-020	1693	9 over 0 or 6 or inverted 9					
	WMSH-025	1693	3 over inverted 2					

95

William III (1695 – 1701)

✓	No.	Date	Features	Grade	Purchased From	Date	Price Paid	Value Now
	W3SH-005	1695						
	W3SH-010	1696	obv. 1					
	W3SH-015	1696	no rev. stops; obv. 1					
	W3SH-020	1696	MAB instead of MAG (rev.); obv. 1					
	W3SH-025	1696	GVLIEMVS instead of GVLIELMVS (obv.); obv. 1					
	W3SH-030	1696	GVLIELM∀S instead of GVLIELMVS (obv.); obv. 1					
	W3SH-035	1669	1669 instead of 1696; obv. 1					
	W3SH-040	1696	PROOF on thick flan; obv. 1					
	W3SH-045	1696	mintmark B; obv. 1					
	W3SH-050	1696	mintmark B; struck over hammered shilling; obv. 1					
	W3SH-055	1696	mintmark C; obv. 1					
	W3SH-060	1696	mintmark C; PROOF on thick flan; obv. 1					
	W3SH-065	1696	mintmark E; obv. 1					
	W3SH-070	1696	mintmark N; obv. 1					
	W3SH-075	1696	mintmark y; obv. 1					
	W3SH-080	1696	mintmark Y; obv. 1					
	W3SH-085	1696	Y over inverted Y (mintmark); obv. 1					
	W3SH-090	1696	obv. 2					
	W3SH-095	1696	mintmark C; obv. 3					
	W3SH-100	1696	mintmark E; obv. 3					
	W3SH-105	1696	mintmark y; obv. 3					
	W3SH-110	1697	obv. 1					
	W3SH-115	1697	Scotland/Ireland shields transposed (rev.); obv. 1					
	W3SH-120	1697	shields rotated clockwise 90 degrees (rev.); obv. 1					
	W3SH-125	1697	no rev. stops; obv. 1					
	W3SH-130	1697	GVLELMVS instead of GVLIELMVS (obv.); obv. 1					
	W3SH-135	1697	GRI instead of GRA (obv.); obv. 1					
	W3SH-140	1697	DE(over A)I instead of DEI (obv.); obv. 1					
	W3SH-145	1697	mintmark B; obv. 1					
	W3SH-150	1697	mintmark C; obv. 1					
	W3SH-155	1697	mintmark C; Scotland/Ireland shields transposed (rev.); obv. 1					
	W3SH-160	1697	mintmark E; obv. 1					
	W3SH-165	1697	mintmark N; obv. 1					
	W3SH-170	1697	mintmark y; obv. 1					
	W3SH-175	1697	mintmark y; France/Ireland shields transposed (rev.); obv. 1					
	W3SH-180	1697	mintmark y; Scotland/Ireland shields transposed (rev.); obv. 1					
	W3SH-185	1697	mintmark Y; obv. 1					
	W3SH-190	1697	obv. 3					
	W3SH-195	1697	mintmark B; obv. 3					
	W3SH-200	1697	mintmark C; obv. 3					

Cont.

Shilling

✓	No.	Date	Features	Grade	Purchased From	Date	Price Paid	Value Now
	W3SH-205	1697	mintmark C; no rev. stops; obv. 3					
	W3SH-210	1697	mintmark C; Scotland shield at date; obv. 3					
	W3SH-215	1697	mintmark E; obv. 3					
	W3SH-220	1697	mintmark N; obv. 3					
	W3SH-225	1697	mintmark y; obv. 3					
	W3SH-230	1697	obv. 4					
	W3SH-235	1697	GVLIELM∇S instead of GVLIELMVS (obv.); obv. 4					
	W3SH-240	1697	mintmark B; obv. 4					
	W3SH-245	1697	mintmark C; obv. 4					
	W3SH-250	1697	mintmark C; struck on thick flan					
	W3SH-255	1698	obv. 4					
	W3SH-260	1698	PROOF; edge plain; obv. 4					
	W3SH-265	1698	plumes on rev.; obv. 4					
	W3SH-270	1698	obv. 5					
	W3SH-275	1698	PROOF; edge plain; obv. 5					
	W3SH-280	1699	obv. 5					
	W3SH-285	1699	struck on thick flan; obv. 5					
	W3SH-290	1699	obv. 6					
	W3SH-295	1699	PROOF; edge plain; obv. 6					
	W3SH-300	1699	plumes on rev.; obv. 6					
	W3SH-305	1699	roses on rev.; obv. 6					
	W3SH-310	1700						
	W3SH-315	1700	plume below head					
	W3SH-320	1701						
	W3SH-325	1701	plumes on rev.					

Anne   (1702 – 1714)

Before Union of England and Scotland

✓	No.	Date	Features	Grade	Purchased From	Date	Price Paid	Value Now
	ASH-005	1702						
	ASH-010	1702	plumes on rev.					
	ASH-015	1702	VIGO below head					
	ASH-020	1703	VIGO below head					
	ASH-025	1704						
	ASH-030	1704	plumes on rev.					
	ASH-035	1705						
	ASH-040	1705	plumes on rev.					
	ASH-045	1705	roses and plumes on rev.					
	ASH-050	1707	roses and plumes on rev.					

After Union of England and Scotland

✓	No.	Date	Features	Grade	Purchased From	Date	Price Paid	Value Now
	ASH-055	1707	E below head; obv. 2					
	ASH-060	1707	E below head; PROOF; edge plain; obv. 2					
	ASH-065	1707	E* below head; obv. 2					
	ASH-070	1707						
	ASH-075	1707	plumes on rev.					

Cont.

Coincraft's Coin Checklist

✓	No.	Date	Features	Grade	Purchased From	Date	Price Paid	Value Now
	ASH-080	1707	E below head; obv. 3					
	ASH-085	1707	E* below head; obv. 4					
	ASH-090	1708	E below head; obv. 2					
	ASH-095	1708	E* below head; obv. 2					
	ASH-100	1708	8 over 7; obv. 2					
	ASH-105	1708	roses and plumes on rev.; obv. 2					
	ASH-110	1708	obv. 3					
	ASH-115	1708	plumes on rev.; obv. 3					
	ASH-120	1708	roses and plumes on rev.; obv. 3					
	ASH-125	1708	E below head; obv. 3					
	ASH-130	1708	E below head; 8 over 7; obv.3					
	ASH-135	1708	E* below head; obv. 4					
	ASH-140	1709	obv. 3					
	ASH-145	1709	ANNA over DEI (obv.); obv. 3					
	ASH-150	1709	IIIB instead of HIB (rev.); obv. 3					
	ASH-155	1709	E* below head; obv. 4					
	ASH-160	1709	E* below head; rev. ↑; obv. 4					
	ASH-165	1710	roses and plumes on rev.; obv. 3					
	ASH-170	1710	PROOF; edge plain; obv. 5					
	ASH-175	1710	roses and plumes on rev.; obv. 5					
	ASH-180	1710	PROOF; edge plain roses and plumes on rev.; obv. 5					
	ASH-185	1711	obv. 3					
	ASH-190	1711	obv. 5					
	ASH-195	1712	roses and plumes on rev.					
	ASH-200	1713	3 over 2 roses and plumes on rev.					
	ASH-205	1714	roses and plumes on rev.					
	ASH-210	1714	roses and plumes on rev. inverted 'L' instead of 'I' (both) in obv. legend					
	ASH-215	1714	4 over 3					

George I (1714 – 1727)

✓	No.	Date	Features	Grade	Purchased From	Date	Price Paid	Value Now
	G1SH-005	1715	roses and plumes on rev.					
	G1SH-010	1716	roses and plumes on rev.					
	G1SH-015	1717	roses and plumes on rev.					
	G1SH-020	1718	roses and plumes on rev.					
	G1SH-025	1719	roses and plumes on rev.					
	G1SH-030	1720	roses and plumes on rev.					
	G1SH-035	1720	roses and plumes on rev.; edge plain					
	G1SH-040	1720	(plain in angles)					
	G1SH-045	1721	(plain in angles)					
	G1SH-050	1721	roses and plumes on rev.					
	G1SH-055	1721	plumes and roses on rev. (i.e. reversed positions)					
	G1SH-058	1721	plumes and roses on rev. (i.e. reversed positions); 21 over 18					
	G1SH-060	1721	latter 1 over 0; roses and plumes on rev.					
	G1SH-065	1721	21 over 19 or 18 roses and plumes on rev.					

Cont.

Shilling

✓	No.	Date	Features	Grade	Purchased From	Date	Price Paid	Value Now
	G1SH-070	1722	roses and plumes on rev.					
	G1SH-075	1723	roses and plumes on rev.					
	G1SH-080	1723	SS C in angles; obv. 1					
	G1SH-085	1723	SS C in angles with one C over SS; obv. 1					
	G1SH-090	1723	SS C in angles arms of France at date; obv. 1					
	G1SH-095	1723	SS C in angles; obv. 2					
	G1SH-100	1723	roses and plumes on rev.; obv. 2					
	G1SH-105	1723	WCC below head; plumes and interlinked 'C's on rev.; obv. 2					
	G1SH-110	1724	roses and plumes on rev.					
	G1SH-115	1724	WCC below head; plumes and interlinked 'C's on rev.					
	G1SH-120	1725	roses and plumes on rev.					
	G1SH-125	1725	roses and plumes on rev.; no stops on obv.					
	G1SH-130	1725	WCC below head; plumes and interlinked 'C's on rev.					
	G1SH-135	1726	roses and plumes on rev.					
	G1SH-140	1726	WCC below head; plumes and interlinked 'C's on rev.					
	G1SH-145	1727	roses and plumes on rev.					
	G1SH-150	1727	roses and plumes on rev.; no stops on obv.					

George II (1727 – 1760)

✓	No.	Date	Features	Grade	Purchased From	Date	Price Paid	Value Now
	G2SH-005	1727	plumes on rev.					
	G2SH-010	1727	roses and plumes on rev.					
	G2SH-015	1728						
	G2SH-020	1728	roses and plumes on rev.					
	G2SH-025	1728	roses and plumes on rev.; E of GEOR over R (obv.)					
	G2SH-030	1729	roses and plumes on rev.					
	G2SH-035	1731	roses and plumes on rev.					
	G2SH-040	1731	plumes on rev.					
	G2SH-045	1732	roses and plumes on rev.					
	G2SH-050	1734	roses and plumes on rev.					
	G2SH-055	1735	roses and plumes on rev.					
	G2SH-060	1736	roses and plumes on rev.					
	G2SH-065	1736	6 over 5 roses and plumes on rev.					
	G2SH-070	1737	roses and plumes on rev.					
	G2SH-075	1739	roses on rev.					
	G2SH-080	1739	9 over 7; roses on rev.					
	G2SH-085	1739	unusually small Garter star (rev.); roses on rev.					
	G2SH-090	1741	roses on rev.					
	G2SH-095	1743	roses on rev.					
	G2SH-100	1743	3 over 1 roses on rev.					
	G2SH-105	1745	roses on rev.					
	G2SH-110	1745	5 over 3 roses on rev.					

Cont.

Coincraft's Coin Checklist

✓	No.	Date	Features	Grade	Purchased From	Date	Price Paid	Value Now
	G2SH-115	1745	LIMA below head					
	G2SH-118	1745	LIMA below head; A of LIMA unbarred					
	G2SH-120	1746	LIMA below head					
	G2SH-125	1746	6 over 5 LIMA below head					
	G2SH-130	1746	PROOF					
	G2SH-135	1747	roses on rev.					
	G2SH-140	1747	latter 7 over 6; roses on rev.					
	G2SH-145	1750	oval '0' in date					
	G2SH-150	1750	oval '0' over 6					
	G2SH-155	1750	5 over 4; round '0' in date					
	G2SH-160	1750	50 over 46; oval '0' in date					
	G2SH-165	1751						
	G2SH-170	1758						

George III (1760 – 1820)

✓	No.	Date	Features	Grade	Purchased From	Date	Price Paid	Value Now
	G3SH-005	1763						
	G3SH-010	1787	rev. 2					
	G3SH-015	1787	1 over reversed 1; rev. 2					
	G3SH-020	1787	PROOF on thick flan; edge plain; rev. 2					
	G3SH-025	1787	no stop over head; rev. 2					
	G3SH-030	1787	no stop over head PROOF; rev. 2					
	G3SH-035	1787	no stop over head PROOF; edge plain; rev. 2					
	G3SH-040	1787	no stop over head PROOF on thick flan; edge plain; rev. 2					
	G3SH-045	1787	no stops on obv.; rev. 2					
	G3SH-050	1787	no stops on obv. PROOF; edge plain; rev. 2					
	G3SH-055	1787	no stops at date; rev. 2					
	G3SH-060	1787	latter 7 over 6; no stops at date; rev. 2					
	G3SH-065	1787	rev. 3					
	G3SH-070	1787	1 over reversed 1; rev. 3					
	G3SH-075	1787	PROOF; rev. 3					
	G3SH-080	1787	PROOF on thick flan; edge plain; rev. 3					
	G3SH-085	1798						

Sixpence

Oliver Cromwell (Commonwealth 1649 – 1660)

✓	No.	Date	Features	Grade	Purchased From	Date	Price Paid	Value Now
	CR6D-005	1658						

Charles II (1660 – 1685)

✓	No.	Date	Features	Grade	Purchased From	Date	Price Paid	Value Now
	C26DM-005	1674						
	C26DM-010	1675						
	C26DM-015	1675	5 over 4					
	C26DM-020	1676	latter 6 usually over 5					
	C26DM-025	1677						
	C26DM-030	1678	8 always over 7					
	C26DM-035	1679						
	C26DM-040	1680						
	C26DM-045	1681						
	C26DM-050	1682						
	C26DM-055	1682	2 over 1					
	C26DM-060	1683						
	C26DM-065	1684						

James II (1685 – 1688)

✓	No.	Date	Features	Grade	Purchased From	Date	Price Paid	Value Now
	J26D-005	1686						
	J26D-010	1686	8 over 6					
	J26D-015	1687	rev. 1					
	J26D-020	1687	7 over 6; rev. 1					
	J26D-025	1687	rev. 2					
	J26D-030	1687	rev. 3					
	J26D-035	1687	7 over 6; rev. 3					
	J26D-040	1688						

William & Mary (1688 – 1694)

✓	No.	Date	Features	Grade	Purchased From	Date	Price Paid	Value Now
	WM6D-005	1693						
	WM6D-010	1693	3 of date inverted (see note below)					
	WM6D-015	1694						

Coincraft's Coin Checklist

William III (1695 – 1701)

✓	No.	Date	Features	Grade	Purchased From	Date	Price Paid	Value Now
	W36D-005	1695						
	W36D-010	1696	obv. 1; rev. 1					
	W36D-015	1696	latter 6 over 5; obv. 1; rev. 1					
	W36D-020	1696	no stops on obv.; obv. 1; rev. 1					
	W36D-025	1696	shield of Scotland at date; obv. 1; rev. 1					
	W36D-030	1696	shield of France at date; obv. 1; rev. 1					
	W36D-035	1696	struck on thick flan; obv. 1; rev. 1					
	W36D-040	1696	mintmark B; obv. 1; rev. 1					
	W36D-045	1696	mintmark C; obv. 1; rev. 1					
	W36D-050	1696	mintmark E; obv. 1; rev. 1					
	W36D-055	1696	mintmark N; obv. 1; rev. 1					
	W36D-060	1696	mintmark y; obv. 1; rev. 1					
	W36D-065	1696	mintmark Y; obv. 1; rev. 1					
	W36D-070	1696	mintmark Y; no stops on obv.; obv. 1; rev. 1					
	W36D-075	1696	obv. 1; rev. 2					
	W36D-080	1696	no stops on rev.; obv. 1; rev. 2					
	W36D-085	1696	obv. 1; rev. 3					
	W36D-090	1696	mintmark B; obv. 1; rev. 2					
	W36D-095	1696	mintmark B; no stops on obv.					
	W36D-100	1696	mintmark B; obv. 1; rev. 3					
	W36D-105	1696	mintmark B; no stops on obv.					
	W36D-110	1696	mintmark C; obv. 1; rev. 3					
	W36D-115	1696	mintmark E; obv. 1; rev. 3					
	W36D-120	1696	mintmark N; obv. 1; rev. 3					
	W36D-125	1696	obv. 2; rev. 3					
	W36D-130	1696	GVLELMVS instead of GVLIELMVS (obv.); obv. 2; rev. 3					
	W36D-135	1696	mintmark Y; obv. 3; rev. 2					
	W36D-140	1696	mintmark E; obv. 3; rev. 2					
	W36D-145	1697	obv. 1; rev. 3					
	W36D-150	1697	Arms of France and Ireland transposed; obv. 1; rev. 3					
	W36D-155	1697	GVLIELM∇S instead of GVLIELMVS (obv.); obv. 1; rev. 3					
	W36D-160	1697	struck on shilling blank; obv. 1; rev. 3					
	W36D-165	1697	mintmark B; obv. 1; rev. 2					
	W36D-170	1697	mintmark B; obv. 1; rev. 3					
	W36D-172	1697	mintmark B; rev. ↑; obv. 1; rev. 3					
	W36D-175	1697	mintmark B; reads M.AG on rev.; extra stops after FRA & HIB; obv. 1; rev. 3					
	W36D-180	1697	mintmark C; obv. 1; rev. 2					
	W36D-185	1697	mintmark C; obv. 1; rev. 3					
	W36D-190	1697	mintmark C; shield of Ireland at date; obv. 1; rev. 3					
	W36D-195	1697	mintmark E; obv. 1; rev. 2					
	W36D-200	1697	mintmark E; obv. 1; rev. 3					
	W36D-205	1697	E over B (mintmark); obv. 1; rev. 3					

Cont.

Sixpence

✓	No.	Date	Features	Grade	Purchased From	Date	Price Paid	Value Now
	W36D-210	1697	mintmark N; obv. 1; rev. 3					
	W36D-215	1697	mintmark N; rev. ↑; obv. 1; rev. 3					
	W36D-220	1697	mintmark N; GVLIEMVS instead of GVLIELMVS (obv.); obv. 1; rev. 3					
	W36D-225	1697	mintmark y; obv. 1; rev. 3					
	W36D-230	1697	mintmark y; tiny 7 in date; obv. 1; rev. 3					
	W36D-235	1697	mintmark y; shield of Ireland at date; obv. 1; rev. 3					
	W36D-240	1697	obv. 2; rev. 3					
	W36D-245	1697	GVLIEMVS instead of GVLIELMVS (obv.); obv. 2; rev. 3					
	W36D-250	1697	obv. 3; rev. 2					
	W36D-255	1697	GVLIEIMVS instead of GVLIELMVS (obv.); obv. 3; rev. 2					
	W36D-260	1697	G∀LIELMVS instead of GVLIELMVS (obv.); obv. 3; rev. 2					
	W36D-265	1697	obv. 3; rev. 3					
	W36D-270	1697	mintmark B; obv. 3; rev. 2					
	W36D-275	1697	mintmark B; IRA instead of FRA (obv.); obv. 3; rev. 2					
	W36D-280	1697	mintmark C; obv. 3; rev. 2					
	W36D-285	1697	mintmark C; obv. 3; rev. 3					
	W36D-290	1697	mintmark E; obv. 3; rev. 2					
	W36D-295	1697	mintmark E; obv. 3; rev. 3					
	W36D-300	1697	mintmark Y; obv. 3; rev. 3					
	W36D-305	1698						
	W36D-310	1698	plumes on rev.					
	W36D-315	1699						
	W36D-320	1699	plumes on rev.					
	W36D-325	1699	roses on rev.					
	W36D-330	1699	roses on rev. G∀LIELMVS instead of GVLIELMVS (obv.)					
	W36D-335	1700						
	W36D-340	1700	plume below head					
	W36D-345	1701						

Anne (1702 – 1714)

Before Union of England and Scotland

✓	No.	Date	Features	Grade	Purchased From	Date	Price Paid	Value Now
	A6D-005	1703	VIGO below head					
	A6D-010	1705						
	A6D-015	1705	plumes on rev.; rev. 1					
	A6D-020	1705	plumes on rev.; rev. 2					
	A6D-025	1705	roses and plumes on rev.					
	A6D-030	1707	roses and plumes on rev.					

After Union of England and Scotland

✓	No.	Date	Features	Grade	Purchased From	Date	Price Paid	Value Now
	A6D-035	1707	rev. 3					
	A6D-040	1707	rev. 4					
	A6D-045	1707	E below head					

Cont.

Coincraft's Coin Checklist

✓	No.	Date	Features	Grade	Purchased From	Date	Price Paid	Value Now
	A6D-050	1707	PROOF; edge plain E below head					
	A6D-055	1707	plumes on rev.					
	A6D-060	1708						
	A6D-065	1708	E below head					
	A6D-070	1708	8 over 7; E below head					
	A6D-075	1708	E* below head; obv. 1					
	A6D-080	1708	8 over 7; E* below head					
	A6D-085	1708	E* below head; obv. 2					
	A6D-090	1708	plumes on rev.					
	A6D-095	1710	roses and plumes on rev.					
	A6D-100	1711	rev. 3					
	A6D-105	1711	rev. 5					

George I (1714 – 1727)

✓	No.	Date	Features	Grade	Purchased From	Date	Price Paid	Value Now
	G16D-005	1717	roses and plumes on rev.					
	G16D-010	1717	edge plain; roses and plumes on rev.					
	G16D-015	1720	20 always over 17 roses and plumes on rev.					
	G16D-020	1723	SSC in angles on rev.					
	G16D-025	1726	roses and plumes on rev.					

George II (1727 – 1760)

✓	No.	Date	Features	Grade	Purchased From	Date	Price Paid	Value Now
	G26D-005	1728						
	G26D-010	1728	PROOF; edge plain					
	G26D-015	1728	plumes on rev.					
	G26D-020	1728	roses and plumes on rev.					
	G26D-025	1731	roses and plumes on rev.					
	G26D-030	1732	roses and plumes on rev.					
	G26D-035	1734	roses and plumes on rev.					
	G26D-040	1735	roses and plumes on rev.					
	G26D-045	1735	5 over 4; roses and plumes on rev.					
	G26D-050	1736	roses and plumes on rev.					
	G26D-055	1739	roses on rev.					
	G26D-060	1739	O in GEORGIVS over R (obv.)					
	G26D-065	1741	roses on rev.					
	G26D-070	1743	roses on rev.					
	G26D-075	1745	roses on rev.					
	G26D-080	1745	5 over 3 roses on rev.					
	G26D-085	1745	LIMA below head					
	G26D-090	1746	LIMA below head					
	G26D-095	1746	PROOF					
	G26D-100	1750						
	G26D-105	1751						
	G26D-110	1757						
	G26D-115	1758						

Cont.

Sixpence

✓	No.	Date	Features	Grade	Purchased From	Date	Price Paid	Value Now
	G26D-120	1758	8 over 7					

George III (1760 – 1820)

✓	No.	Date	Features	Grade	Purchased From	Date	Price Paid	Value Now
	G36D-005	1787	rev. 1					
	G36D-010	1787	PROOF; edge plain					
	G36D-015	1787	PROOF on thick flan; edge plain					
	G36D-020	1787	rev. 2					

Maundy Fourpence

Charles II (1660 – 1685)

✓	No.	Date	Features	Grade	Purchased From	Date	Price Paid	Value Now
	C24MM-005	none						
	C24MM-010	1670						
	C24MM-015	1671						
	C24MM-020	1672	2 over 1					
	C24MM-025	1673						
	C24MM-030	1674						
	C24MM-035	1674	7 over 6					
	C24MM-040	1674	4 over horizontal 4					
	C24MM-045	1675						
	C24MM-050	1675	5 over 4					
	C24MM-055	1676						
	C24MM-060	1676	7 over 6					
	C24MM-065	1676	latter 6 over 5					
	C24MM-070	1677						
	C24MM-075	1678						
	C24MM-080	1678	8 over 6					
	C24MM-085	1678	8 over 7					
	C24MM-090	1679						
	C24MM-095	1680						
	C24MM-100	1681						
	C24MM-105	1681	B of HIB over R (rev.)					
	C24MM-110	1681	1 over 0					
	C24MM-115	1682						
	C24MM-120	1682	2 over 1					
	C24MM-125	1683						
	C24MM-130	1684						
	C24MM-135	1684	4 over 3					

James II (1685 – 1688)

✓	No.	Date	Features	Grade	Purchased From	Date	Price Paid	Value Now
	J24M-005	1686						
	J24M-010	1686	date nearer top of crown					
	J24M-015	1687	7 over 6					
	J24M-020	1687	7 over 6; 8 over 7					
	J24M-025	1688						
	J24M-030	1688	1 over 8					
	J24M-035	1688	latter 8 over 7					

William & Mary (1688 – 1694)

✓	No.	Date	Features	Grade	Purchased From	Date	Price Paid	Value Now
	WM4M-005	1689						

Cont.

Maundy Fourpence

✓	No.	Date	Features	Grade	Purchased From	Date	Price Paid	Value Now
	WM4M-010	1690						
	WM4M-015	1690	6 over 5					
	WM4M-020	1691						
	WM4M-025	1691	1 over 0					
	WM4M-030	1692						
	WM4M-035	1692	2 over 1					
	WM4M-040	1693						
	WM4M-045	1693	3 over 2					
	WM4M-050	1694	obv. 1					
	WM4M-055	1694	obv. 2					

William III (1695 – 1701)

✓	No.	Date	Features	Grade	Purchased From	Date	Price Paid	Value Now
	W34M-005	1697						
	W34M-010	1698						
	W34M-015	1699						
	W34M-020	1700						
	W34M-025	1701						
	W34M-030	1702						

Anne (1702 – 1714)

✓	No.	Date	Features	Grade	Purchased From	Date	Price Paid	Value Now
	A4M-005	1703						
	A4M-010	1704						
	A4M-015	1705						
	A4M-020	1706						
	A4M-025	1708						
	A4M-030	1709						
	A4M-035	1710						
	A4M-040	1713						

George I (1714 – 1727)

✓	No.	Date	Features	Grade	Purchased From	Date	Price Paid	Value Now
	G14M-005	1717						
	G14M-010	1721						
	G14M-015	1723						
	G14M-020	1727						

George II (1727 – 1760)

✓	No.	Date	Features	Grade	Purchased From	Date	Price Paid	Value Now
	G24M-005	1729						
	G24M-010	1731						
	G24M-015	1732						

Cont.

Coincraft's Coin Checklist

✓	No.	Date	Features	Grade	Purchased From	Date	Price Paid	Value Now
	G24M-020	1735						
	G24M-025	1737						
	G24M-030	1739						
	G24M-035	1740						
	G24M-040	1743						
	G24M-045	1743	3 over 0					
	G24M-050	1746						
	G24M-055	1760						

George III (1760 – 1820)

✓	No.	Date	Features	Grade	Purchased From	Date	Price Paid	Value Now
	G34M-005	1763						
	G34M-010	1763	PROOF; rev. ↑					
	G34M-015	1765						
	G34M-020	1765	E in GEORGIVS over R (obv.)					
	G34M-025	1766						
	G34M-030	1770						
	G34M-035	1772						
	G34M-040	1772	2 over 0					
	G34M-045	1776						
	G34M-050	1780						
	G34M-055	1784						
	G34M-060	1786						
	G34M-065	1792						
	G34M-070	1795						
	G34M-075	1800						

Silver Threepence

Charles II (1660 – 1685)

✓	No.	Date	Features	Grade	Purchased From	Date	Price Paid	Value Now
	C23MM-005	none						
	C23MM-010	1670						
	C23MM-015	1671						
	C23MM-020	1671	first A in GRATIA inverted					
	C23MM-025	1671	first A in GRATIA unbarred					
	C23MM-030	1672	2 over 1					
	C23MM-035	1673						
	C23MM-040	1674						
	C23MM-045	1675						
	C23MM-050	1676						
	C23MM-055	1676	latter 6 over 5					
	C23MM-060	1676	ERA instead of FRA (rev.)					
	C23MM-065	1677						
	C23MM-070	1678						
	C23MM-075	1679						
	C23MM-080	1679	O of CAROLVS over A (obv.)					
	C23MM-085	1680						
	C23MM-090	1681						
	C23MM-095	1681	latter 1 over 0					
	C23MM-100	1682						
	C23MM-105	1682	2 over 1					
	C23MM-110	1683						
	C23MM-115	1684						
	C23MM-120	1684	4 over 3					

James II (1685 – 1688)

✓	No.	Date	Features	Grade	Purchased From	Date	Price Paid	Value Now
	J23M-005	1685						
	J23M-010	1685	die axes at 90 degrees					
	J23M-015	1685	struck on fourpence flan					
	J23M-020	1686						
	J23M-025	1687						
	J23M-030	1687	7 over 6					
	J23M-035	1688						
	J23M-040	1688	latter 8 over 7					

William & Mary (1688 – 1694)

✓	No.	Date	Features	Grade	Purchased From	Date	Price Paid	Value Now
	WM3M-005	1689						
	WM3M-010	1689	rev. stops are hyphens					
	WM3M-015	1689	GVLIE(LMV over MVS)S (obv.)					

Cont.

Coincraft's Coin Checklist

✓	No.	Date	Features	Grade	Purchased From	Date	Price Paid	Value Now
	WM3M-020	1689	no stops on rev.					
	WM3M-025	1690						
	WM3M-030	1690	6 over 5					
	WM3M-035	1690	9 over 6 or inverted 9					
	WM3M-040	1690	9 over 6 or inverted 9; BR FR over BB FB (rev.)					
	WM3M-045	1691	obv. 1					
	WM3M-050	1691	obv. 2					
	WM3M-055	1692						
	WM3M-060	1693						
	WM3M-065	1693	3 over 2					
	WM3M-070	1694						
	WM3M-075	1694	MΛRIΛ instead of MARIA (obv.)					

William III (1695 – 1701)

✓	No.	Date	Features	Grade	Purchased From	Date	Price Paid	Value Now
	W33M-005	1698						
	W33M-010	1699						
	W33M-015	1700						
	W33M-020	1701	Z-type '1's in date					
	W33M-025	1701	Z-type '1's in date; GBA instead of GRA (obv.)					
	W33M-030	1701	J-type '1's in date					

Anne (1702 – 1714)

✓	No.	Date	Features	Grade	Purchased From	Date	Price Paid	Value Now
	A3M-005	1703						
	A3M-010	1704						
	A3M-015	1705						
	A3M-020	1706						
	A3M-025	1707						
	A3M-030	1708						
	A3M-035	1709						
	A3M-040	1710						
	A3M-045	1713	obv. 1					
	A3M-050	1713	obv. 2					

George I (1714 – 1727)

✓	No.	Date	Features	Grade	Purchased From	Date	Price Paid	Value Now
	G13M-005	1717						
	G13M-010	1721						
	G13M-015	1723						
	G13M-020	1727						

Silver Threepence

George II (1727 – 1760)

✓	No.	Date	Features	Grade	Purchased From	Date	Price Paid	Value Now
	G23M-005	1729						
	G23M-010	1731						
	G23M-015	1731	small obverse lettering					
	G23M-020	1732	no stop over head					
	G23M-025	1732	stop over head					
	G23M-030	1735						
	G23M-035	1737						
	G23M-040	1739						
	G23M-045	1740						
	G23M-050	1743	large obv. and rev. lettering					
	G23M-055	1743	small lettering no stop over head					
	G23M-060	1743	small lettering stop over head					
	G23M-065	1746						
	G23M-070	1746	6 over 3 or 5					
	G23M-075	1760						

George III (1760 – 1820)

✓	No.	Date	Features	Grade	Purchased From	Date	Price Paid	Value Now
	G33M-005	1762						
	G33M-010	1763						
	G33M-015	1763	PROOF; rev. ↑					
	G33M-020	1765						
	G33M-025	1766						
	G33M-030	1770						
	G33M-035	1772	small lettering					
	G33M-040	1772	large lettering; large III					
	G33M-045	1772	large lettering; small III					
	G33M-050	1780						
	G33M-055	1784						
	G33M-060	1786						
	G33M-065	1792						
	G33M-070	1795						
	G33M-075	1800						

Silver Twopence

Charles II   (1660 – 1685)

✓	No.	Date	Features	Grade	Purchased From	Date	Price Paid	Value Now
	C22MM-005	none						
	C22MM-010	1668	unusual rev. ↑ as stated					
	C22MM-015	1670						
	C22MM-020	1671						
	C22MM-025	1672	2 over 1					
	C22MM-030	1673						
	C22MM-035	1674						
	C22MM-040	1675						
	C22MM-045	1676						
	C22MM-050	1677						
	C22MM-055	1678						
	C22MM-060	1678	8 over 6					
	C22MM-065	1679						
	C22MM-070	1679	struck on large flan					
	C22MM-075	1679	HIB over FRA (rev.)					
	C22MM-080	1680						
	C22MM-085	1680	80 over 79					
	C22MM-090	1681						
	C22MM-095	1682						
	C22MM-100	1682	2 over 1					
	C22MM-105	1682	2 over 1 ERA instead of FRA (rev.)					
	C22MM-110	1683						
	C22MM-115	1683	3 over 2					
	C22MM-120	1684						

James II   (1685 – 1688)

✓	No.	Date	Features	Grade	Purchased From	Date	Price Paid	Value Now
	J22M-005	1686						
	J22M-010	1686	IΛCOBVS instead of IACOBVS (obv.)					
	J22M-015	1687						
	J22M-020	1687	ERA instead of FRA (rev.)					
	J22M-025	1688						
	J22M-030	1688	latter 8 over 7					

William & Mary   (1688 – 1694)

✓	No.	Date	Features	Grade	Purchased From	Date	Price Paid	Value Now
	WM2M-005	1689						
	WM2M-010	1691						
	WM2M-015	1692						
	WM2M-020	1693						
	WM2M-025	1693	3 over 2					

Cont.

Silver Twopence

✓	No.	Date	Features	Grade	Purchased From	Date	Price Paid	Value Now
	WM2M-030	1694						
	WM2M-035	1694	4 over 3					
	WM2M-040	1694	MARLA instead of MARIA (obv.)					
	WM2M-045	1694	HI instead of HIB (rev.)					

William III (1695 – 1701)

✓	No.	Date	Features	Grade	Purchased From	Date	Price Paid	Value Now
	W32M-005	1698						
	W32M-010	1699						
	W32M-015	1700						
	W32M-020	1701						

Anne (1702 – 1714)

✓	No.	Date	Features	Grade	Purchased From	Date	Price Paid	Value Now
	A2M-005	1703						
	A2M-010	1704						
	A2M-015	1704	no obverse stops					
	A2M-020	1705						
	A2M-025	1706						
	A2M-030	1707						
	A2M-035	1708						
	A2M-040	1709						
	A2M-045	1710						
	A2M-050	1713						

George I (1714 – 1727)

✓	No.	Date	Features	Grade	Purchased From	Date	Price Paid	Value Now
	G12M-005	1717						
	G12M-010	1721						
	G12M-015	1723						
	G12M-020	1726						
	G12M-025	1727						

George II (1727 – 1760)

✓	No.	Date	Features	Grade	Purchased From	Date	Price Paid	Value Now
	G22M-005	1729						
	G22M-010	1731						
	G22M-015	1732						
	G22M-020	1735						
	G22M-025	1737						
	G22M-030	1739						
	G22M-035	1740						
	G22M-040	1743						

Cont.

Coincraft's Coin Checklist

✓	No.	Date	Features	Grade	Purchased From	Date	Price Paid	Value Now
	G22M-045	1743	3 over 0					
	G22M-050	1746						
	G22M-055	1756						
	G22M-060	1756	large date					
	G22M-065	1759						
	G22M-070	1760						

George III (1760 – 1820)

✓	No.	Date	Features	Grade	Purchased From	Date	Price Paid	Value Now
	G32M-005	1763						
	G32M-010	1763	PROOF; rev. ↑					
	G32M-015	1765						
	G32M-020	1766						
	G32M-025	1772						
	G32M-030	1772	second 7 over 6					
	G32M-035	1776						
	G32M-040	1780						
	G32M-045	1784						
	G32M-050	1786						
	G32M-055	1792						
	G32M-060	1795						
	G32M-065	1800						

Copper Twopence

George III (1760 – 1820)

✓	No.	Date	Features	Grade	Purchased From	Date	Price Paid	Value Now
	G32D-005	1797						
	G32D-010	1797	PROOF					
	G32D-015	1797	bronzed PROOF					
	G32D-020	1797	gilt PROOF					
	G32D-025	1797	Late Soho issue; PROOF					
	G32D-030	1797	Late Soho issue; PROOF on thin flan					
	G32D-035	1797	Late Soho issue; bronzed PROOF					
	G32D-040	1797	Late Soho issue; bronzed PROOF on thin flan					
	G32D-045	1797	Late Soho issue; gilt PROOF					
	G32D-050	1797	Late Soho issue; gilt PROOF on thin flan					
	G32D-055	1797	PROOF in silver					
	G32D-060	1797	PROOF in silver on thin flan					
	G32D-065	1797	PROOF in gold					

Silver Penny

Charles II (1660 – 1685)

✓	No.	Date	Features	Grade	Purchased From	Date	Price Paid	Value Now
	C21MM-005	none						
	C21MM-010	1670						
	C21MM-015	1671						
	C21MM-020	1672	2 over 1					
	C21MM-025	1673						
	C21MM-030	1674						
	C21MM-035	1674	G of GRATIA inverted (obv.)					
	C21MM-040	1674	as last but GRACIA instead of GRATIA					
	C21MM-045	1675						
	C21MM-050	1676						
	C21MM-055	1676	G of GRATIA inverted (obv.)					
	C21MM-060	1677						
	C21MM-065	1677	G of GRATIA inverted (obv.)					
	C21MM-070	1678						
	C21MM-075	1678	G of GRATIA inverted (obv.)					
	C21MM-080	1679						
	C21MM-085	1680						
	C21MM-090	1680	struck on larger thin flan					
	C21MM-095	1681						
	C21MM-100	1682						
	C21MM-105	1682	2 over 1					
	C21MM-110	1682	ERA instead of FRA (rev.)					
	C21MM-115	1683						
	C21MM-120	1684						
	C21MM-125	1684	4 over 3					

James II (1685 – 1688)

✓	No.	Date	Features	Grade	Purchased From	Date	Price Paid	Value Now
	J21M-005	1685						
	J21M-010	1686						
	J21M-015	1687						
	J21M-020	1687	7 over 6					
	J21M-022	1687	7 over 8					
	J21M-025	1688						
	J21M-030	1688	latter 8 over 7					

William & Mary (1688 – 1694)

✓	No.	Date	Features	Grade	Purchased From	Date	Price Paid	Value Now
	WM1M-005	1689						
	WM1M-010	1689	GVIELMVS instead of GVLIELMVS (obv.)					

Cont.

Silver Penny

✓	No.	Date	Features	Grade	Purchased From	Date	Price Paid	Value Now
	WM1M-015	1690						
	WM1M-020	1691	latter 1 over 0					
	WM1M-025	1692						
	WM1M-030	1692	2 over 1					
	WM1M-035	1693						
	WM1M-040	1694	stops on obv.					
	WM1M-045	1694	no stops on obv.					
	WM1M-050	1694	HI instead of HIB (rev.)					
	WM1M-055	1694	9 over 6 or inverted 9; HI instead of HIB (rev.)					

William III (1695 – 1701)

✓	No.	Date	Features	Grade	Purchased From	Date	Price Paid	Value Now
	W31M-005	1698						
	W31M-010	1698	IRA instead of FRA (rev.)					
	W31M-015	1698	HI.BREX instead of HIB.REX (rev.)					
	W31M-020	1699						
	W31M-025	1700						
	W31M-030	1701						

Anne (1702 – 1714)

✓	No.	Date	Features	Grade	Purchased From	Date	Price Paid	Value Now
	A1M-005	1703						
	A1M-010	1705						
	A1M-015	1706						
	A1M-020	1708						
	A1M-025	1709						
	A1M-030	1710						
	A1M-035	1713	3 over 0					

George I (1714 – 1727)

✓	No.	Date	Features	Grade	Purchased From	Date	Price Paid	Value Now
	G11M-005	1716						
	G11M-010	1718						
	G11M-015	1720						
	G11M-020	1720	HIPEX or HIPREX instead of HIB REX (rev.)					
	G11M-025	1723						
	G11M-030	1725						
	G11M-035	1726						
	G11M-040	1727						

Coincraft's Coin Checklist

George II (1727 – 1760)

✓	No.	Date	Features	Grade	Purchased From	Date	Price Paid	Value Now
	G21M-005	1729						
	G21M-010	1731						
	G21M-015	1732						
	G21M-020	1735						
	G21M-025	1737						
	G21M-030	1739						
	G21M-035	1740						
	G21M-040	1743						
	G21M-045	1746						
	G21M-050	1746	6 over 3 (?)					
	G21M-055	1750						
	G21M-060	1752						
	G21M-065	1752	2 over 0					
	G21M-070	1753						
	G21M-075	1753	3 over 2					
	G21M-080	1754						
	G21M-085	1755						
	G21M-090	1756						
	G21M-095	1757	no colon after GRATIA (obv.)					
	G21M-100	1757	colon after GRATIA (obv.)					
	G21M-105	1758						
	G21M-110	1759						
	G21M-115	1760						

George III (1760 – 1820)

✓	No.	Date	Features	Grade	Purchased From	Date	Price Paid	Value Now
	G31M-005	1763						
	G31M-010	1763	PROOF; rev. ↑					
	G31M-015	1766						
	G31M-020	1770						
	G31M-025	1772						
	G31M-030	1776						
	G31M-035	1779						
	G31M-040	1780						
	G31M-045	1781						
	G31M-050	1784						
	G31M-055	1786						
	G31M-060	1792						
	G31M-065	1795						
	G31M-070	1800						

Copper/Bronze Penny

George III (1760 – 1820)

✓	No.	Date	Features	Grade	Purchased From	Date	Price Paid	Value Now
	G31D-005	1797						
	G31D-010	1797	Late Soho issue; PROOF					
	G31D-015	1797	Late Soho issue; bronzed PROOF					
	G31D-020	1797	Late Soho issue; gilt PROOF					
	G31D-025	1797	Late Soho issue; silvered PROOF					
	G31D-030	1797	Late Soho issue; PROOF in tin					
	G31D-035	1797	Late Soho issue; PROOF in silver					
	G31D-040	1797	Late Soho issue; PROOF in silver on thin flan					
	G31D-045	1797	Late Soho issue; PROOF in gold					
	G31D-050	1806						
	G31D-055	1806	gilt PROOF					
	G31D-058	1806	gilt PROOF; rev. ↑					
	G31D-060	1806	PROOF					
	G31D-065	1806	PROOF on thin flan; edge plain					
	G31D-070	1806	bronzed PROOF; rev. ↑					
	G31D-072	1806	bronzed PROOF					
	G31D-075	1806	bronzed PROOF; edge plain					
	G31D-080	1806	bronzed PROOF on thin flan; edge plain					
	G31D-085	1806	gilt PROOF					
	G31D-090	1806	gilt PROOF; edge plain					
	G31D-095	1806	gilt PROOF on thin flan; edge plain					
	G31D-100	1806	PROOF in silver; edge plain					
	G31D-105	1807						
	G31D-110	1807	bronzed PROOF					
	G31D-115	1807	gilt PROOF					
	G31D-120	1808						

Halfpenny

Charles II (1660 – 1685)

✓	No.	Date	Features	Grade	Purchased From	Date	Price Paid	Value Now
	C2HDM-005	1672						
	C2HDM-010	1672	CRAOLVS instead of CAROLVS (obv.)					
	C2HDM-015	1672	PROOF					
	C2HDM-020	1672	PROOF in silver					
	C2HDM-025	1673						
	C2HDM-030	1673	No stops on obv.					
	C2HDM-035	1673	No stop on rev.					
	C2HDM-040	1673	CRAOLVS instead of CAROLVS (obv.)					
	C2HDM-045	1673	PROOF					
	C2HDM-050	1673	PROOF in silver					
	C2HDM-055	1675						
	C2HDM-060	1675	5 over 3					
	C2HDM-065	1675	No stops on obv.					

James II (1685 – 1688)

✓	No.	Date	Features	Grade	Purchased From	Date	Price Paid	Value Now
	J2HD-005	1685						
	J2HD-010	1685	no star between NVMMORVM and FAMVLVS					
	J2HD-015	1686						
	J2HD-020	1687						

William & Mary (1688 – 1694)

✓	No.	Date	Features	Grade	Purchased From	Date	Price Paid	Value Now
	WMHD-005	1689	obv. 1; rev. 1					
	WMHD-010	(1689)	PROOF, plain edge; obv. 1; rev. 1					
	WMHD-015	1689	obv. 1; rev. 2					
	WMHD-020	1689	obv. 2; rev. 1					
	WMHD-025	1690						
	WMHD-030	1691	edge date 1691					
	WMHD-035	1691	edge date 1692					
	WMHD-040	1692						
	WMHD-045	1694						
	WMHD-050	1694	GVLEELMVS instead of GVLIELMVS (obv.)					
	WMHD-055	1694	GVLIEMVS instead of GVLIELMVS (obv.)					
	WMHD-060	1694	MVRIA instead of MARIA (obv.)					
	WMHD-065	1694	MΛRIΛ instead of MARIA (obv.)					
	WMHD-070	1694	BRITΛNNIΛ (last I over Λ) instead of BRITANNIA (rev.)					
	WMHD-072	1694	BRTΛNNIΛ instead of BRITANNIA (rev.)					

Cont.

Halfpenny

✓	No.	Date	Features	Grade	Purchased From	Date	Price Paid	Value Now
	WMHD-075	1694	no stop on rev.					
	WMHD-080	1694	PROOF					
	WMHD-085	1694	PROOF, edge striated					
	WMHD-090	1694	PROOF on thin flan					
	WMHD-095	1694	PROOF in silver					
	WMHD-100	1694	PROOF in silver on thin flan					
	WMHD-105	1694	PROOF in gold on thin flan					

William III (1694 – 1701)

✓	No.	Date	Features	Grade	Purchased From	Date	Price Paid	Value Now
	W3HD-005	1695						
	W3HD-010	1695	struck on thick flan					
	W3HD-015	1696						
	W3HD-020	1696	GVLIEMVS instead of GVLIELMVS (obv.)					
	W3HD-025	1696	TERTVS instead of TERTIVS (obv.)					
	W3HD-030	1696	PROOF in silver					
	W3HD-035	1696	PROOF in silver on thin flan					
	W3HD-040	1697						
	W3HD-045	1697	I of TERTIVS over E (obv.)					
	W3HD-050	1697	GVLILMVS instead of GVLIELMVS (obv.)					
	W3HD-055	1697	gap instead of first N in BRITANNIA					
	W3HD-060	1698	rev. 1					
	W3HD-065	no date	double headed					
	W3HD-070	1698	rev. 2					
	W3HD-075	1699	obv. 1; rev. 2					
	W3HD-080	1699	GVLIEMVS instead of GVLIELMVS (obv.) obv. 1; rev. 2					
	W3HD-085	1699	obv. 2; rev. 3					
	W3HD-090	1699	GVILELMVS instead of GVLIELMVS (obv.); obv. 2; rev. 3					
	W3HD-095	1699	TERTVS instead of TERTIVS (obv.); obv. 2; rev. 3					
	W3HD-100	1699	PROOF in silver					
	W3HD-105	1700						
	W3HD-110	1700	GVLIELMS instead of GVLIELMVS (obv.)					
	W3HD-115	1700	GVLIEEMVS instead of GVLIELMVS (obv.)					
	W3HD-120	1700	I of TERTIVS over V (obv.)					
	W3HD-125	1700	TER TIVS instead of TERTIVS (obv.)					
	W3HD-130	1700	BRIVANNIA instead of BRITANNIA (obv.)					
	W3HD-135	1701						
	W3HD-140	1701	PROOF in silver					
	W3HD-145	no date	double headed					

Coincraft's Coin Checklist

George I (1714 – 1727)

✓	No.	Date	Features	Grade	Purchased From	Date	Price Paid	Value Now
	G1HD-005	1717						
	G1HD-010	1717	no stops on obv.					
	G1HD-015	1717	PROOF					
	G1HD-020	1717	PROOF in silver					
	G1HD-022	1717	PROOF in silver; rev. ↑					
	G1HD-025	1718						
	G1HD-028	1718	R in BRITANNIA over B					
	G1HD-030	1718	no stops on obv.					
	G1HD-035	1718	in silver					
	G1HD-038	1718	struck on Irish Gun money piece dated 1689					
	G1HD-040	1719	obv. 1					
	G1HD-045	1719	diagonally grained edge; obv. 1					
	G1HD-050	1719	obv. 2					
	G1HD-055	1719	diagonally grained edge; obv. 2					
	G1HD-060	1719	obv. 3					
	G1HD-065	1719	diagonally grained edge; obv. 3					
	G1HD-070	1720						
	G1HD-075	1721						
	G1HD-080	1721	latter 1 over 0					
	G1HD-085	1721	stop after date					
	G1HD-090	1721	struck on 3mm thick flan					
	G1HD-095	1722						
	G1HD-100	1722	GEORGI∀S instead of GEORGIVS					
	G1HD-105	1722	PROOF in brass; rev. ↑					
	G1HD-110	1723						
	G1HD-115	1723	no stop on rev.					
	G1HD-120	1723	struck on thin flan					
	G1HD-125	1724						

George II (1727 – 1760)

✓	No.	Date	Features	Grade	Purchased From	Date	Price Paid	Value Now
	G2HD-005	1729	stop after legend (rev.)					
	G2HD-010	1729	no stop after legend (rev.)					
	G2HD-015	1729	PROOF					
	G2HD-020	1729	PROOF in silver					
	G2HD-025	1729	PROOF in silver on thick flan					
	G2HD-030	1730						
	G2HD-035	1730	GEOGIVS instead of GEORGIVS (obv.)					
	G2HD-040	1731	stop after legend (rev.)					
	G2HD-045	1731	no stop after legend (rev.)					
	G2HD-050	1732						
	G2HD-055	1732	no stop after legend (rev.)					
	G2HD-060	1732	on thick wide flan					
	G2HD-065	1733						
	G2HD-070	1734						

Cont.

Halfpenny

✓	No.	Date	Features	Grade	Purchased From	Date	Price Paid	Value Now
	G2HD-072	1734	R in GEORGIVS over O (obv.)					
	G2HD-075	1734	4 over 3					
	G2HD-080	1734	no stops on obv.					
	G2HD-085	1735						
	G2HD-090	1736						
	G2HD-095	1737						
	G2HD-100	1738						
	G2HD-105	1738	V in GEORGIVS over S (obv.)					
	G2HD-110	1739						
	G2HD-115	1740						
	G2HD-120	1742						
	G2HD-125	1742	2 over 0					
	G2HD-130	1743						
	G2HD-135	1744						
	G2HD-140	1745						
	G2HD-145	1746						
	G2HD-150	1747						
	G2HD-155	1748						
	G2HD-160	1749						
	G2HD-165	1750						
	G2HD-170	1751						
	G2HD-175	1752						
	G2HD-180	1753						
	G2HD-185	1754						

George III (1760 – 1820)

✓	No.	Date	Features	Grade	Purchased From	Date	Price Paid	Value Now
	G3HD-005	1770						
	G3HD-010	1770	no stop on rev.					
	G3HD-015	1770	PROOF					
	G3HD-020	1770	PROOF in silver					
	G3HD-025	1771						
	G3HD-030	1771	no stop on rev.					
	G3HD-035	1772						
	G3HD-040	1772	GEORIVS instead of GEORGIVS (obv.)					
	G3HD-045	1772	no stop on rev.					
	G3HD-050	1773						
	G3HD-055	1773	no stop after REX (obv.)					
	G3HD-060	1773	no stop on rev.					
	G3HD-065	1774						
	G3HD-070	1775						
	G3HD-075	1799						
	G3HD-080	1799	PROOF					
	G3HD-082	1799	gilt PROOF					
	G3HD-085	1806						
	G3HD-090	1806	PROOF edge grained					
	G3HD-095	1806	gilt PROOF edge grained					
	G3HD-100	1807						

Farthing

Charles II (1660 – 1685)

✓	No.	Date	Features	Grade	Purchased From	Date	Price Paid	Value Now
	C2FAM-005	1672						
	C2FAM-006	1672	A of CAROLVS over B (obv.)					
	C2FAM-007	1672	RO of CAROLO over OL (obv.)					
	C2FAM-008	1672	rev. ↑					
	C2FAM-010	1672	no stops on obv.					
	C2FAM-012	1672	no stop on rev.					
	C2FAM-015	1673						
	C2FAM-020	1673	CAROLA instead of CAROLO (obv.)					
	C2FAM-025	1673	BRITINNIA instead of BRITANNIA (rev.)					
	C2FAM-030	1673	no stops on obv.					
	C2FAM-035	1673	no stop on rev.					
	C2FAM-040	1674						
	C2FAM-045	1675						
	C2FAM-048	1675	5 over 2 or 3					
	C2FAM-050	1675	no stop after CAROLVS (obv.)					
	C2FAM-055	1679						
	C2FAM-060	1679	no stop on rev.					
	C2FAM-065	1684						
	C2FAM-070	1685						

James II (1685 – 1688)

✓	No.	Date	Features	Grade	Purchased From	Date	Price Paid	Value Now
	J2FA-005	1684						
	J2FA-010	1685						
	J2FA-015	1685	no copper plug					
	J2FA-020	1686						
	J2FA-025	1687	obv. 1					
	J2FA-030	1687	obv. 2					

William & Mary (1688 – 1694)

✓	No.	Date	Features	Grade	Purchased From	Date	Price Paid	Value Now
	WMFA-005	1689	edge date 1689					
	WMFA-010	1689	PROOF in copper; edge plain					
	WMFA-015	1689	edge date 1690					
	WMFA-020	1690	edge date 1689					
	WMFA-025	1690	edge date 1690					
	WMFA-028	1690	edge date 1691					
	WMFA-030	1690	PROOF in copper; edge plain					
	WMFA-035	1691						
	WMFA-040	1692						

Cont.

Farthing

✓	No.	Date	Features	Grade	Purchased From	Date	Price Paid	Value Now
	WMFA-045	1693						
	WMFA-050	1694						
	WMFA-055	1694	struck on thick wide flan					
	WMFA-060	1694	GVLIELMS instead of GVLIELMVS (obv.)					
	WMFA-065	1694	PROOF					
	WMFA-070	1694	PROOF in silver					

William III (1694 – 1701)

✓	No.	Date	Features	Grade	Purchased From	Date	Price Paid	Value Now
	W3FA-005	1695						
	W3FA-010	1695	struck on thick flan					
	W3FA-015	1695	GVLIELMV instead of GVLIELMVS (obv.)					
	W3FA-020	1695	M in GVLIELMVS over V (obv.)					
	W3FA-025	1695	PROOF in silver					
	W3FA-030	1696						
	W3FA-035	1696	PROOF in silver					
	W3FA-040	1697						
	W3FA-045	1697	GVLIELMS instead of GVLIELMVS (obv.)					
	W3FA-050	1697	TERTIV instead of TERTIVS (obv.)					
	W3FA-055	1697	PROOF in silver					
	W3FA-060	1698	rev. 1					
	W3FA-065	1698	B of BRITANNIA over G (rev.); rev. 1					
	W3FA-070	1698	rev. 2					
	W3FA-075	1698	PROOF in silver; rev. 2					
	W3FA-080	1699	rev. 1					
	W3FA-085	1699	GVLILEMVS instead of GVLIELMVS (obv.); rev. 1					
	W3FA-088	1699	I in TERTIVS over V (obv.); rev. 1					
	W3FA-090	1699	rev. 2					
	W3FA-095	1699	PROOF in silver; rev. 2					
	W3FA-100	1699	PROOF in silver on thick flan; rev. 2					
	W3FA-105	1700						
	W3FA-110	1700	GVLILMVS instead of GVLIELMVS (obv.)					
	W3FA-112	1700	BBITANNIA instead of BRITANNIA (rev.)					
	W3FA-115	1700	RRITANNIA instead of BRITANNIA (rev.)					
	W3FA-120	1700	R of BRITANNIA over B					
	W3FA-125	1700	rev. ↑					
	W3FA-130	1700	PROOF in silver					
	W3FA-135	none	struck on wide flan					

Anne (1701 – 1714)

✓	No.	Date	Features	Grade	Purchased From	Date	Price Paid	Value Now
	AFA-005	1714						

Coincraft's Coin Checklist

George I (1714 – 1727)

✓	No.	Date	Features	Grade	Purchased From	Date	Price Paid	Value Now
	G1FA-005	1717						
	G1FA-010	1717	PROOF					
	G1FA-015	1717	PROOF on thick flan					
	G1FA-020	1717	PROOF in silver; rev. ↑					
	G1FA-025	1717	PROOF in silver on thin flan					
	G1FA-030	1718	PROOF in silver on thin flan					
	G1FA-035	1719						
	G1FA-036	1719	no rev. linear circle; very small 9 in date					
	G1FA-037	1719	very small 9 in date					
	G1FA-038	1719	very large 9 in date					
	G1FA-039	1719	latter A in BRITANNIA over I					
	G1FA-040	1719	struck on 25mm diameter flan					
	G1FA-045	1719	obv. legend continues over head					
	G1FA-050	1719	in silver					
	G1FA-055	1720						
	G1FA-060	1720	edge vertically milled					
	G1FA-065	1720	edge vertically milled; struck on thin flan					
	G1FA-070	1721						
	G1FA-075	1721	latter 1 over 0					
	G1FA-080	1722						
	G1FA-085	1723						
	G1FA-090	1723	R of REX over horizontal R					
	G1FA-095	1724						
	G1FA-100	none	struck on 5 mm thick flan			•		

George II (1727 – 1760)

✓	No.	Date	Features	Grade	Purchased From	Date	Price Paid	Value Now
	G2FA-005	1730						
	G2FA-010	1730	PROOF					
	G2FA-015	1730	PROOF in silver					
	G2FA-020	1730	PROOF in silver on thick flan; rev. ↑					
	G2FA-025	1731						
	G2FA-030	1732						
	G2FA-032	1732	2 over 1					
	G2FA-035	1733						
	G2FA-040	1734						
	G2FA-045	1734	no stops on obv.					
	G2FA-050	1735						
	G2FA-055	1735	3 double-struck					
	G2FA-060	1735	3 double-struck; struck on thick flan					
	G2FA-065	1736						
	G2FA-070	1737						
	G2FA-075	1737	large date					
	G2FA-080	1739						
	G2FA-085	1739	9 over 5					

Cont.

Farthing

✓	No.	Date	Features	Grade	Purchased From	Date	Price Paid	Value Now
	G2FA-090	1741						
	G2FA-095	1744						
	G2FA-100	1746						
	G2FA-105	1746	V of GEORGIVS over U (obv.)					
	G2FA-110	1749						
	G2FA-115	1750						
	G2FA-120	1754						
	G2FA-125	1754	4 over 0					

George III (1760 – 1820)

✓	No.	Date	Features	Grade	Purchased From	Date	Price Paid	Value Now
	G3FA-005	1771						
	G3FA-008	1771	first 7 over 1					
	G3FA-010	1771	PROOF					
	G3FA-015	1773						
	G3FA-020	1773	no stop on rev.					
	G3FA-025	1773	no stop after REX (obv.)					
	G3FA-030	1774						
	G3FA-035	1775						
	G3FA-038	1775	V in GEORGIVS is ∀					
	G3FA-040	1799						
	G3FA-045	1799	PROOF					
	G3FA-050	1799	PROOF; edge plain					
	G3FA-055	1799	Bronzed PROOF					
	G3FA-060	1799	Bronzed PROOF; edge plain					
	G3FA-065	1799	gilt PROOF					
	G3FA-070	1799	gilt PROOF; edge plain					
	G3FA-075	1799	PROOF in silver; edge plain					
	G3FA-080	1799	PROOF in gold; edge plain					
	G3FA-085	1806						
	G3FA-090	1806	PROOF					
	G3FA-095	1806	Bronzed PROOF					
	G3FA-100	1806	Bronzed PROOF; edge plain					
	G3FA-105	1806	gilt PROOF					
	G3FA-110	1806	gilt PROOF; edge plain					
	G3FA-115	1806	PROOF in silver; edge plain					
	G3FA-120	1806	PROOF in gold; edge plain					
	G3FA-125	1807						

Proof Set

George II (1727 – 1760)

1746

✓	No.	Date	Features	Grade	Purchased From	Date	Price Paid	Value Now
	PS-1746	1746	Proof					